FRESH START

Fresh Start

Overcoming Chronic Disorganization And Hoarding Group Mannual

For those who treat clients with hoarding behaviors and chronic disorganization: A psychotherapy group manual to facilitate change and improve quality of life.

Barbara Jo Dennison PhD, LISW-S

Karen Kruzan LISW-S, CPO-CD

ISBN: 978-1-62249-216-9

Published by The Educational Publisher Inc.

Biblio Publishing

BiblioPublishing.com

TABLE OF CONTENTS

Contents

PREFACE

When we first began working with the chronically disorganized and hoarding populations, there was little research and even fewer treatment models for this population. Our first group in 2010 was with six brave women who agreed to participate in a four week psychotherapy group we developed. Based largely on their feedback and that of subsequent groups, the eight-week Fresh Start Program was born. We knew from our individual psychotherapy and professional organizing services that this population was extremely isolated, fearful of others finding out about their struggles, and desperately in need of a way to change. To date we have conducted nine groups and have two more scheduled. It has been extremely rewarding to be let into our clients homes, into their suffering, and to watch them grow. The changes that our Fresh Start graduates have made are truly inspiring and we admire them.

Karen Kruzan, LISW-S, CPO-CD
Barbara Jo Dennison, PhD, LISW-S

Praise for Fresh Start: Overcoming Chronic Disorganization and Hoarding Group Manual

Going to Fresh Start group has been life-saving for me...not in a physical "CPR" kind of way, but in an emotional day-to-day "live life to its fullest" kind of way! I became aware of the group during individual therapy, and the combination of the two have been instrumental in the progress I am making as I deal with my chronic disorganization. While I had problems prior to my husband's sudden and unexpected death, everything got worse after he died. After experiencing such an incredible loss, which 11 years later is still hard for me to accept, *I found myself bringing more stuff into my house than I ever took out...leaving no room for living any kind of "normal" life.*

My three adult children have been incredibly patient and understanding, beyond what anyone in their situations should have to bear. They are grieving, too. (They lost their paternal grandfather in January, and their father in July of the same calendar year.) We all experienced deep losses, and we have all grieved in our own way. I am embarrassed that these three remarkable individuals have developed their own relationships with significant others, in spite of the fact my house has been too awful to have these people visit. My two daughters-in-law, and my daughter's boyfriend have never set foot in my house. This has to stop! But *before Fresh Start, I really did not care...now I do!*

I think that enduring the deep loss of my wonderful husband has made me want to hang on to everything else in my life because I don't want to lose anyone, or anything else. My computer files are as full as my paper files and piles of stuff in my house...my pattern of not letting go is everywhere!!

The Fresh Start Group helped me realize that I am not alone, and that there is a light at the end of the tunnel. The group leaders and members *respect and understand* each other, which is so helpful. Not feeling judged, or lazy, or uncaring, or unclean, is also extremely important in the healing process. Having the opportunity to share stories, experiences, and even let go of actual "stuff" with others who are in similar situations has been of incredible support and benefit for me. I feel so alone in my personal life without my husband, but now I know that I am not alone as I face the task of getting rid of the stuff in my life.

Another group member and I have exchanged phone numbers in addition to the mutual email addresses we shared in the group. By "accident" at the first meeting, we realized we had some mutual friends... we talked about where we were from while waiting for the group to start and started sharing names. She and I seem to have "connected" in our similar situations and we offer additional support via email, phone, and have met before a group session just to talk.

I am very grateful to Dr. Joey and Karen for this incredible group. Their professional experiences and incredible knowledge, combined with their very pleasant and easy-going personalities are the perfect mix for a successful group! Thanks!!

Diane M., Fresh Start Graduate

The *Fresh Start Group Manual* offers a wealth of practical and easy to digest information. While not shying away from the complex nature of the conditions, hope and possibility for relief spring from the pages as the authors convey a judgment-free, person-centered, and competency-rich collaborative treatment model. The manual will quickly broaden the world view, sensitivity and engagement strategy of the clinician exposed to chronic disorganization and hoarding behaviors for the first time and is a must-have for clinicians and programs ready to take the next step in providing innovative group treatment services.

Kappy Madenwald, LISW-S
Madenwald Consulting, LLC

This manual and the therapy groups are a useful tool for helping CD and hoarding clients reclaim their homes. There is nothing as powerful as the "me too" especially when many of these clients have lost supporting relationships often as a result of the clutter. Included are recommended inventories, and scales to help group members and therapist assess stressors, assess the clutter severity. It also helps clients develop a productive language to discuss the challenges of deciding where to begin, negative thinking, and feelings of being overwhelmed when progress is slow. Thanks for sharing this valuable tool Karen and Dr. Dennison!

Melanie Dennis, CPO

ACKNOWLEDGEMENTS

We are grateful to all of our clients who, over 30 years of practice have taught us strength and resiliency in the face of traumatic life situations.

We could not have developed this the Fresh Start Group program without our families who graciously supported us as we developed, ran, and revised the group format. They were there to listen to our successes and frustrations as we put together this manual. We will be forever grateful for all they gave up to help us achieve our dream of bringing this manual to you.

Thank you to our clients who allowed us to photograph their homes and use those photos to help others learn about chronic disorganization and hoarding.

Thank you to our photographer, Amy Elizabeth for creating the cover photo of a group session as well as the photo used to open Chapter Two. We appreciate your work in capturing on film the work we do.

About the Authors

Karen Kruzan, LISW-S, CPO-CD

has spent the past 25 years changing lives. She is the owner of K^2 Organizing, and provides individual therapy, group therapy, and professional organizing to people who are overwhelmed by clutter and disorganization. Ms. Kruzan has been published in the ICD's *Guide to Collaborating with Professional Organizers: For Related Professionals*, presented across the country on hoarding, and produced a training video for those working with people who hoard. She was twice the featured organizer on TLC's Hoarding: Buried Alive. Ms. Kruzan is a Hoarding and Chronic Disorganization Specialist, as well as a member of National Association of Social Workers (NASW), Institute for Challenging Disorganization (ICD), and National Association of Professional Organizers (NAPO).

Barbara Jo Dennison PhD, LISW-S

received her doctorate in psychology from California Southern University and her undergraduate and graduate degrees in social work from The Ohio State University. She is the owner of Dennison & Associates, Inc. a wellness firm in Powell, Ohio. She has served as a field instructor for Capital University and for The Ohio State University. She has over 30 years of professional experience working with families in crisis situations, and first responders after traumatic events. In the early 80,s she was trained in the trauma based technique of Critical Incident Stress Management. She is a certified EMDR therapist and hypnotherapist. In 2005, she wrote a white paper on the Treatments for Secondary Traumatic Stress and lectures on how to become resilient after traumatic events change life. In 2013 she recorded a professional training DVD on "The Many Faces of Hoarding and Trauma". She was a featured psychotherapist on TLC's Hoarding Buried Alive T V show.

Dr. Dennison is a professional member of: National Association of Social Workers, Eye Movement Desensitization Reprocessing International Association, Institute for Hypnotherapy, Institute For Challenging Disorganization, International Society for Traumatic Stress Studies, National Association of Professional Women and a board member for The Powell Chamber of Commerce.

She is a published author, has developed a greeting card line of gratitude cards, recorded a "Meditations of Gratitude" CD sold on Amazon.com. Four times per year, she provides a day retreat; teaching coping mechanisms to mitigate the effects of primary and secondary stress for helping professionals.

PART 1

Introduction

"To be happy at home is the ultimate result of all ambition."

Samuel Johnson

A widow cannot face being home alone and she prides herself on finding good deals. She acquires more craft supplies than she can use or store, rendering her craft room unusable.

A married woman moved to the house next door from her husband because there was no room for both her and her husband's stuff.

A married mother of two can't see the clutter in her home because when she does, she becomes overwhelmed by anxiety that leads her to dissociate. She avoids the situation by shopping for good deals.

A young woman refuses to invite friends over because of the state of her apartment. Her attempts to tackle the problem have led her to give up when faced with even a decision about where to start.

An older woman is trying to dig out of her hoarded home, but she is unwilling to let go of anything "pretty".

We encounter people in similar situations every day, and most people have no idea how common they are. The people we have met along the journey to write this book have taught us that they desire to be happy with their living spaces and to calm the chaos in their brains. They are, for the most part, very ambitious with their desires to change. But, (there is a big BUT) there are biological, psychological, and environmental challenges that lock them in patterns of trying to change, failing and losing hope that life could ever be any better. People with chronic disorganization and/or hoarding behaviors view their belongings in the same ways as people who are not struggling with chronic disorganization (CD) or hoarding. The difference lies in the strengths of the beliefs and feelings about their stuff (we use the word "stuff" to describe the various items people have in their possession so as to avoid listing those items or judging their worth) and the perceived need to avoid the intense emotions related to dealing with it. We propose that when people are working so hard to organize the chaos in their lives, their minds, bodies, and spirits are in perpetual states of fight, flight, or freeze.

Our hope is that this book will assist behavioral health professionals and professional organizers in their quest to deliver quality group experiences for people suffering with chronic disorganization and/or hoarding. This is a "how to" text. In the first portion of this book you will learn about the historical view of hoarding, including the emergence of the DSM-5 hoarding diagnostic classification, and the role that trauma plays in the chaos. Chapters One through Nine will provide you with a step by step guide to deliver evidence-based techniques from cognitive behavioral therapy, mindfulness, and hypnotherapy in a psychotherapy group for this population. The Leader's Guide at the end of the book and the participants' pages on CD are provided to help you begin running the Fresh Start Program.

Background of Hoarding

According to Samuels et al. 2008, between one and three million people in the United States experience a lifelong struggle with acquiring and holding on to nearly everything they acquire. (Digging Out, page 1) According to the DSM-5 the prevalence of hoarding disorder in the United States and Europe is approximately 2%-6%. There are other accounts that indicate currently between 15 and 16 million people in the U.S. suffer from hoarding disorder. The National Alliance on Mental Illness (NAMI) reports up to 5% of the world population displays clinical hoarding features. There are people whose living situations are not dire and they often go unnoticed until the situation is out of control. Some people become so severely affected that they live in unsafe or unsanitary living conditions. Their lifestyles and health are compromised to the point of losing the interest of family members, isolation from neighbors and community, and work and legal ramifications. People who hoard often face threats of eviction, potential loss of custody of their children, and actions from the Health Department or Zoning Commission. Before the emergence of the DSM-5, Tolin, Frost, Steketee, 1996 provided this helpful definition of hoarding:

1. The accumulation and great difficulty getting rid of objects that others would generally believe have little value

2. The clutter is so severe it prevents or limits living/working spaces

3. The clutter, acquiring, or difficulty discarding causes significant distress or impairment

In 2013 The American Psychiatric Association released the DSM-5, which now includes the diagnostic criteria for Hoarding Disorder. This publication indicates that at this time, hoarding is viewed as a chronic condition. It defines six criteria that must be met in order to diagnose 300.3, Hoarding Disorder. These criteria, like those above from Tolin, Frost, and Steketee, require difficulty discarding, a significant amount of clutter, and distress or impairment. Before diagnosing Hoarding Disorder, clinicians need to familiarize themselves with all the DSM-5 criteria, including the differential diagnoses and specifiers.

The DSM-5 states that most people (80%-90%) have difficulty with excessive acquisition, most commonly acquiring possessions by buying them. Bringing home free items and stealing are less common forms of the acquiring seen in Hoarding Disorder.

Hoarding behaviors usually begin in childhood or adolescence (11-15), with excessive saving or collecting. The problem often goes unnoticed due to parental efforts to limit access to items typically hoarded and/or by purging excess. Confused and frustrated parents can, in their efforts to be helpful and curb the behaviors, convey the message that hoarding behaviors are shameful and thus to be kept private. The disorder can run in families and is more prevalent in males (Jack F. Samuels, 2008), with 50 being the average age of a person who hoards. The DSM-5 indicates that in clinical samples hoarding symptoms are more prevalent in females. Perhaps this is because traditionally, more females than males enter therapy. There is ongoing research to develop specific genetic markers to determine who may be affected.

Hoarding disorder is three times more prevalent in older adults (55-94) than in people between ages 34 and 44. This may be due to the time required to accumulate enough stuff to cause distress or impairment, along with the decreasing ability to physically organize and/or purge possessions.

The hoarded home is often marked by pathways through rooms, piles of important and unimportant items mixed together, and areas that are no longer serving the purpose for which they were originally intended. For example, a shower curtain rod may serve as a coat hanger, the oven may store important documents, and the kitchen table may host a litter box.

Thanks to the prevalence of reality television shows, the awareness of hoarding and its consequences continues to grow. This type of media exposure can become a yardstick by which to measure one's struggle with clutter. Some watch the shows to reassure themselves that they are "not *that* bad", or to keep them from becoming "*that* bad". Some research estimates that 10 million Americans suffer from hoarding, but what about the millions of Americans who do not meet the DSM-5 definition of hoarding?

Chronic disorganization, a term coined by Judith Kohlberg[1], likely affects even more Americans than does hoarding. Chronic Disorganization (CD) has three defining features:

- Severe disorganization over an extended period of time
- Daily undermining of quality of life due to the disorganization
- A history of failed self-help attempts with little expectation of improvement without outside assistance

Common characteristics of people struggling with chronic disorganization include:

- Accumulation of significantly more items than necessary
- Difficulty discarding items
- Struggles with mail and paper management
- Multiple incomplete projects
- Challenges with time awareness
- Distractibility
- Wide range of interests
- Difficulty with decision making
- Over-reliance on visual cues

Some people who are chronically disorganized are living with ADHD, depression, anxiety, chronic fatigue syndrome, or other issues. We will discuss some of these health and behavioral health challenges in Chapter X. In our work with the chronically disorganized, we encounter intelligent, creative, compassionate, and engaging people who are highly critical of themselves. They are often afraid that they will be seen as having a hoarding problem or are on their way to having one.

We include this information on chronic disorganization because it is a condition just beginning to get attention outside of the world of professional organizers. It is helpful for psychotherapists to recognize this common associated feature in many diagnoses so that it can become part of the intervention plan.

Many Views of the Problem

Adaptive forms of hoarding behaviors have existed since the beginning of time. For example, history tells us that pharos were buried in pyramids with their possessions. In addition to these items being needed in the afterlife, this could have been an indication that these things were an extension of 'self'. Later in history, hunters and gathers went out into the wilderness and obtained what they anticipated their families would need to hold them over throughout cold winters, droughts or other anticipated upcoming tragedies. Hoarding seemed to be a necessary behavior ages ago to ensure survival. Early man had multiple, creative uses and re-uses for most things in their world. During periods of extreme economic distress, people become adept at ensuring that every last use had been obtained from an item, whether the owner used it himself or passed it on to someone else in need. And then there are the superstitious among us who believe that a certain possession carries a measure of good luck, making parting with those items particularly challenging. Another view is that some people have consistent difficulties making decisions. This in itself may be a problem, but when coupled with a belief that making *the* perfect decision is the only option, to the potential for hoarding increases.

Some assign a sentimental value to objects such that their beliefs are that if they let the objects go, a part of them will actually be lost. This is the idea that we all see things though different schemas, frameworks of beliefs, or views of the world. If a person's schema is that items hold memories, he will believe that getting rid of something also means that the memory will be gone. A person who believes that if she finds pansies especially pretty, for example, she must acquire everything she sees that has a pansy on it. Encompassed in these views are emotional attachments, beliefs about the self in the world, rationales to acquire, and an avoidance of looking at the real reason to keep things.

Psychotherapy Group Intervention

There are many therapeutic options for working with people battling chronic disorganization and hoarding, and the psychotherapy group model described here is one from our toolkit. Our psychotherapy groups for those struggling with chronic disorganization or hoarding bring together people of various ages, socioeconomic status, situation severity, and diagnoses. The group operates under a structured, time-limited model that we created and refined since we started in 2010. The beauty of our model is that it can be run by one therapist, two therapists, or a therapist and professional organizer (PO). In our case, each of us could lead the psychotherapy group individually and it would be more lucrative to do so. There are three reasons why we don't. First, we each have areas of expertise and compatible but different work styles that connect with different clients. Second, dealing alone with the intense emotional interactions of group members can leave one with professional compassion fatigue or burnout. And third, the synergy that comes from the collaboration and joining of behavioral health and organizing is not only good for clients; it fuels us and keeps us coming back for more. Clients in our therapy group benefit from this group model and our collaboration in several key ways:

- Clients who are working with only one of us have the opportunity to "check out" a potential therapist or PO. Many CD clients are uncomfortable with the thought of allowing a stranger into their homes. Having group sessions with a PO and hearing other clients share their stories of what it's like to work with a PO can decrease their anxiety to the point of taking action. Similarly, clients who have negative expectations of individual therapy will often initiate it once they have established trust in the therapist leading the group.
- Clients who are working with both of us outside of group get to see that we are on the same page and that we work well together. That may sound commonplace, but it is often not the case. It is not unusual for there to be territorial battles between a psychotherapist and PO over clients and roles. There can also be animosity if either the therapist or PO believes the other is not doing their share of the work. Instead, clients benefit from a shared treatment plan with no rigid delineation of roles.
- Clients who have other therapists and/or PO's sometimes come to see that CD issues can require a specialized knowledge base that their providers may not have. This is not to say that they should switch from therapists or organizers who are getting results, but that they should treat their chronic disorganization as a serious condition requiring expert care.

Since a therapist can operate a psychotherapy group independently, why would a therapist devote the time and resources necessary to get a collaborative group off the ground?

- The therapist has the opportunity to develop a relationship with a PO and see how she interacts with clients. This first-hand experience is vitally important to have before a therapist makes a referral to someone who will be working with their clients in a situation that is likely to elicit intense emotional reactions. Similarly, the PO can make referrals to a therapist who has demonstrated the knowledge and skills necessary to work with CD clients.

- The therapist does not have to handle the concrete organizing/de-cluttering questions that invariably arise in the psychotherapy group. Instead, they can focus on their area of expertise – behavioral health, and rely on the expertise of, ideally, an Institute for Challenging Disorganization (ICD-trained) professional organizer to address the organizing and de-cluttering challenges.
- Working one-on-one with CD clients can be emotionally draining and sometimes leave a professional questioning their reactions to a client. Collaborating gives both the therapist and PO an opportunity to get a different perspective, as well as share the excitement of successful client experiences.

Our psychotherapy group model, named *Fresh Start: Overcoming Chronic Disorganization*is designed to help members understand the causes and contributing factors to their disorganization, resolve some underlying issues, and instill healthy coping skills and strategies to help them move forward.

As you read the remainder of this publication, it will be easier to follow if you continually refer to the Group Leader's Handbook, found in Part2.

1

GROUP STRUCTURE AND MATERIALS

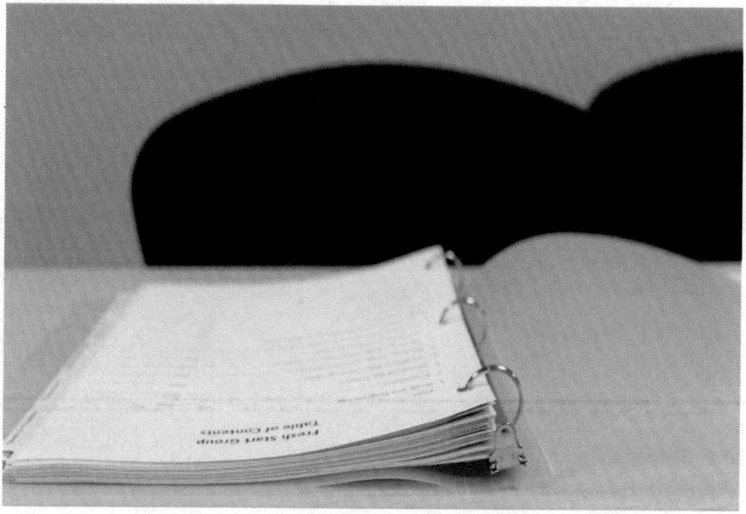
Fresh Start Group
Table of Contents

A. Referrals

Referrals to the Fresh Start group can be generated through many different means, but the easiest method and best way to ensure good group dynamics is using existing clients of the group therapist and/or professional organizer. With existing clients, a diagnostic assessment and/or evaluation of the nature and severity of the disorganization have already occurred.

We do not determine the appropriateness of participation in the Fresh Start Program based on a particular level of clutter or disorganization because we believe that the client's level of distress with their situation and desire to change are better indicators of appropriateness for the program. Existing clients of other therapists and/or professional organizers and self-referrals are also accepted, pending a review of the most recent diagnostic assessment and meeting with the client in their home.

Referred clients who are already in therapy often have completed one or more of the following assessment tools with their therapist. Review of these in addition to the diagnostic evaluation can help the therapist determine the best make-up of members for the group. If the client does not come to you with measures of their present functioning, the following are best practice assessments that are helpful in treatment planning.

- Texas Revised Inventory of Grief Scale is a 21 question self-assessment. It takes 5-10 minutes to complete and score. It gives a perspective of past and present grief reactions.
- Becks Depression Inventory is a multiple choice self-assessment with 21 questions for persons 13 and up. It measures the depth of depression and gives guidance for judging improvement.
- Becks Anxiety Inventory is a 21 question self-assessment multiple choice format. It asks questions regarding symptoms experienced within the previous week to determine between minimal to severe anxiety. The age range is typically 17-80 years old.
- MAST Michigan Alcohol Assessment is a client self-assessment with scoring to assist clients in understanding if alcohol is inhibiting their daily functioning.

- World Health Organization Disability Assessment Schedule (WHODAS) 2.0 from page 747 in the DSM-5.
- DSM-5 Self-Rated Level 1 Cross-Cutting Symptom Measure-Adult on pages 738-739.

B. Materials

Prior to the first group session, group members are given psychotherapy intake paperwork covering the following areas:

- Demographic and Social History
- Billing
- Privacy Notice
- Consent to Treat
- Preparing for Fresh Start Group Psychotherapy – This is a welcoming letter given to members that explains what they can expect in the Fresh Start program. This letter can be found in the Appendix A.

At the first group, members are each given a binder with tabbed dividers and all the agendas/worksheets. Group members are afforded the option of bringing a laptop or tablet that can connect to the internet to download the handouts during the group and work off the electronic copies.

At each group we provide internet access and a hole puncher for any additional handouts distributed during the group session. We upload all materials to www.box.com in a folder only accessible to members in each particular group session. It has been our experience that when we do not provide the materials and a tool for organizing them, we spend valuable group time helping members locate the papers that they need to reference in the group.

All of the materials found in the binders as well as the additional handouts can be found in Part 2 of this manual.

To download copies to print and use in your group along with instructions on making the leader's and group members' binders, go to www.k2organizing.com/FreshStartItems.

C. Overview

Sections

The Fresh Start Program consists of the following eight sections:

- Assessing the Problem
- The Brain's Role: Thinking Patterns
- The Brain's Role: Executive Functions
- The Brain's Role Other Cognitive Factors
- Emotional and Physical Factors
- The Influence of Personality Type: DISC Model
- The Influence of Personality Type: Myers-Briggs Type Indicator
- Moving Forward

Each section roughly corresponds to a ninety minute group session, depending in part on the level of interest and interactivity of the group. The term "section" is used rather than "session" to reflect the flexibility of the program. Sections can overlap weeks and be placed in different sequences, depending on the determination of the group leaders.

Homework

Each week except the last has up to five types of homework assigned:

1. *Section Homework* – Most sections of Fresh Start have homework that is specific to that section, and asks group

members either to dive a little deeper into thinking about a topic or practicing skills discussed in group.

2. *Session evaluation* – To keep things simple, we ask two open-ended questions. These are "What was the best thing about group today?" and "What was the worst thing about group today?" The responses to these questions have helped us shape the group into what it is today, and will continue to make it an even better therapy program. For example, we initially asked members to fill in their responses to those two questions while they were still in the group session. One group member responded that she wanted to be able to complete it as homework because she liked to have a chance to process her thoughts and feelings before writing something that might not accurately or adequately reflect more than a transient thought or emotion. As a result of this feedback, group members can complete these items immediately following each group when it is fresh in their minds, or during the week after they have had time to process the session. You can read more about how we use these session evaluations in Chapter 10.

3. *Clutter-Image Rating Scale*[2] (CIR) uses images to evaluate the level of clutter in various rooms. The images are shown as the assignment is given. Group members are instructed to follow the link where they will see the nine pictures of progressively worsening clutter in each of three rooms. The homework is to record their ratings of their own rooms, evaluating as many rooms as possible. Group members will often become anxious about how they will rate themselves when their rooms do not look like those in the (CIR). They should use their best judgment and focus on the volume of clutter and the impairment on the functionality of the room. We also

suggest to group members that they consider getting a trusted friend or family member to do an independent evaluation using the same tool. This can provide valuable feedback about how others see their homes, as well as prompting important family conversations. If any group member believes that asking another person to do the CIR will lead to excessive or unmanageable distress or conflict, they should not do so. One of the reasons we like the CIR is that many clients lack the ability to see their homes as they really are, judging them to be more or less severely disorganized than they actually are. With the hoarding shows on television and magazines filled with pictures of perfectly organized home spaces, people who are isolated have only two extreme frames of reference. Some will see the magazine photo of a closet with only five outfits and assume that because they have fifteen, they must be hoarding. Others will describe themselves as "not as bad as those people on tv", and thus believe there is not a problem. The CIR shows the full range of clutter and does not assign a value judgment to any rating.

4. *Goal Setting* – This assignment is given every session except the last, and it is to select a small goal that will be completed by the following session. We tell the group that we want them to be successful so they can build on success rather than feel overwhelmed or fail to meet the goals. Group members are asked to share their goals with the group to aid in accountability as well as to ensure that their goals are not too large. The manageability of the goals is primarily determined by how much time there is between group sessions. Some members will need considerable help to set a goal that does not set them up for failure. Other group members are typically very supportive of seemingly minute tasks, recognizing

that fellow group members can get easily overwhelmed and thus not complete their goals. Goal setting is recorded on the Goals and Progress Log found in Part 2.2, where they will not only capture their goals, but also their accomplishments since the previous group session. Additionally, group members will record whether they met their goal and the factors that either led them to success or presented as obstacles.

5. *Activity Homework* – In sessions two and six a unique homework assignment is given, with follow-up homework in sessions three and seven. It is our recommendation that even if the group leader rearranges the sections, the Activity Homework remains in sessions two and six, with the follow-up homework in sessions three and seven. This placement allows enough time in between the activity for group members to make use of the knowledge and skills they have gained in group. This will manifest in growth in their abilities to let go of items, understanding their unhealthy thinking patterns, and process emotions.

Additionally, we choose to keep the Activity Homework out of the binders until weeks two and six when it is assigned. This keeps members who peruse their binders after group one from becoming anxious about the assignment before we can adequately explain it and monitor their reactions.

The Activity is for group members to each think about an item that they will bring to the next group (sessions three and seven). The items should be things that represent their struggles with disorganization, clutter, and/or hoarding. It could be a stapler for someone who has seven and recognizes that they do not need all of them but still cannot let one go. It could be a gift given by a parent that represents a conflicted relationship and is not wanted by the client. It is important to be sure group members are clear about these directions: the items should not have great monetary value, they should be things they would consider donating, throwing out, or selling to a resale shop, and they should be things connected to their struggles with clutter and/or disorganization.

Group leaders need to be prepared and save enough time in group sessions two and six to handle the emotional reactions to this assignment. There is often at least one group member who experiences great anxiety over even the potential that they will be asked to let go of an item. Others will become anxious about choosing the "right" item, and others will seem to have difficulty understanding the assignment even after multiple explanations. All of these reactions need to be addressed in therapeutic discussions so that no member is leaving the group in a state of extreme anxiety or at risk of self-harm. We assure the group members that items will be kept safe in a locked room until the time when they will decide whether to take the items with them or have the group leaders donate them.

When this activity homework is repeated in group six, members should be encouraged to challenge themselves to bring items that are more difficult for them to address than those they brought in week three.

In addition to selecting the items to bring to groups three and six, members will rate their expectations of leaving the items (at least until the following sessions) with the group leaders. These homework questions can be found on the Activity Homework sheet, found in Part 2.19.

The homework for the second and sixth groups was for group members to anticipate how they each would feel about letting an item go and what the outcome would be. The assignment for weeks three and seven is to record how they actually felt and what actually happened as a result. The purpose of repeating this rating assignment is to see if their expectations the second time are more aligned with how they actually felt and what actually happened.

F. Format

The first session begins with evaluation instruments. Each subsequent session begins with group members sharing something that went well since the last group, followed by a review of the homework. As members gather for the start of each group session, the prior week's homework is scanned to become part of their medical records.

After the homework is reviewed and the scanning is completed, the group proceeds onto the section content for the session, and then ends with assignment of homework. This manual will describe each section in the order that we have found most useful.

In terms of completing each week's worksheet, group members need to choose a strategy that is most effective for them. Some members prefer to work on it as the group progresses and while the thoughts are clear to them. Writing can be a way to maximize their attention to the content of the group discussion. Other members become distracted by writing and others want more time to process the information before they write an answer to the question. Each group member is given the option to work on the worksheet either in group or at home in between group sessions.

Each group session ends with an explanation of the homework and goal setting.

2

ASSESSING THE PROBLEM

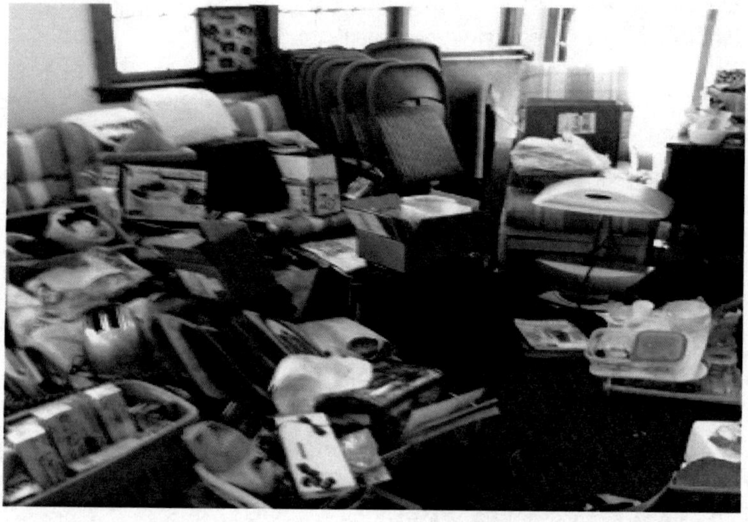

A. Assessments

Group members are given their binders and/or on-line access to the forms as they arrive so they can begin to complete their evaluation instruments. They will complete a variety of assessment tools while they are gathering for the first session and until everyone has had an opportunity to complete them. There are several reasons that we choose to complete the self-assessments during the first group session rather than prior to the session. First, there will always be at least one group member who has completed the assessments prior to group as instructed and at least one who has not. This brings up lots of thoughts and feelings for group members that are not appropriate to discuss in the first meeting. Second, sitting in close proximity to each other without eye contact or dialogue can be helpful to those who are highly anxious because they can become acclimated more slowly to the environment and those around them. Once the interactive portion of the group begins, group members tend to feel more comfortable and thus more likely to share their stories.

There are many options for evaluating the level of acquiring, clutter, and disorganization in homes, and we vary the tools used in each group to best match the makeup of the group. Among the evaluation tools we use are the following:

- Savings Cognitions Inventory[3] is a 24 question tool that asks questions about the thoughts a person has had when deciding whether or not to discard something. This research-based tool evaluates emotional attachment, control, responsibility, and memory.
- Savings Inventory – Revised (Modified Format) is a 23 question self-reporting questionnaire with subscales for clutter, difficulty discarding/saving, and acquisition. There are means for non-clinical samples along with typical scores for people with hoarding problems.
- Hoarding Rating Scale[4,5]is a five question tool that evaluates the major Hoarding Disorder criteria along an eight point scale. The tool provides mean scores for nonclinical samples and people with hoarding problems, along with guidance on determining the clinical significance of hoarding.

- Am I Situationally Disorganized?[6] and Am I Chronically Disorganized?[7] are offered by the Institute for Challenging Disorganization. These two tools are for helping an individual determine the nature of their disorganization. Often this is the first experience a client has with the notion that people are disorganized for different reasons; that even the most organized people can become disorganized after a parent dies and they inherit all or part of the estate.
- ICD Clutter - Hoarding Scale[8] uses a color coded progressive level system that rates an environment on structure and zoning, animals and pests, household functions, health and safety, and personal protective equipment. The ICD considers level III to be the pivot point between a cluttered and a hoarded environment.
- Who Needs Help? Three Ways to Know: Are You an Overshopper[9] invite participants to begin considering the ways in which acquiring and compulsive buying might play a contributing role.

In addition to evaluation acquiring, clutter, and hoarding, we sometimes use trauma rating scales to help determine how group members' behaviors and moods continue to be affected by trauma. Often these scales are used in the diagnostic assessment process prior to the first group session. Whatever clinical choice, the goal is to have the most accurate client information possible in order to better develop client-specific goals.

- Clinician Administered PTSD Scale (CAPS) is the gold standard.It assesses and helps categorize the diagnosis and severity of symptoms, and takes 30 to 60 minutes.
- Acute Stress Disorder Inventory (ASDI) is a 19 question structured interview for diagnosing acute stress disorder and vulnerability to PTSD.

- Acute Stress Disorder Scale is a self-administered version of the ASDI.
- Post-traumatic Stress Disorder Checklist (PCL) is a 17-item self-report scale for PTSD.
- Post-traumatic Symptom Scale - Interview Version (PSS-I) is a semi-structured interview that provides a categorical diagnosis and a measure of the severity of PTSD symptoms.
- Trauma History Scale (THS) is an easy to use self-report measure of exposure to stressors and events that are associated with significant and persistent PTSD.

When group members have completed the assessments, each has the opportunity to introduce herself and share as much or as little as she chooses about her situation and goals for the group. Standard group rules are reviewed, such as protecting the confidentiality of members, allowing each person the opportunity to contribute to the discussion, and respecting differing opinions and lifestyles. As with most therapy groups, there will be members who need more encouragement to speak about their challenges, and others who need to have limits set on the amount of time they are allowed to devote to their story.

Following introductions, the group moves into discussion of the self-rating scales. Typical themes that emerge are:

- I'm not as bad off as I thought I was
- I am worse off than I thought I was
- I am overwhelmed thinking about this
- At least I'm not a shopper

B. Common Characteristics

Educating group members on typical organizing challenges invites sharing of personal stories and decreases the feelings of isolation often experienced by this population. The home of a person with chronic disorganization or hoarding is marked by the accumulation of possessions, and difficulties managing paper is the most common struggle. The person with chronic disorganization may have no remarkable attachment to the items, but is challenging by not knowing what to do with the items they have. Should they be kept, donated, given to friends or family, thrown out, recycled…? If they are kept, how should they be stored? The possibilities seem endless and with no clear solution, items accumulate. For the hoarding client, attachment to possessions can be profound.

Distress with letting go of items is nearly universal. For the CD client, it is sometimes related to emotional attachment, but more commonly related to the anxiety of not knowing the "right" thing to do and the fear of what will happen if they do the "wrong" thing. The hoarding client's distress is typically related to perfectionism, emotional attachment, and fear.

A second common characteristic is the over-reliance on visual cues. Things are left out as reminders of actions to be taken. The problem occurs when there are too many items left out and the actions are not taken. As piles begin to form, the solution of the visual reminder becomes the problem. The person with CD often becomes frustrated and overwhelmed, unable to find a way out of the cycle.

A third characteristic of a person with CD or hoarding is her extensive array of hobbies and interests. A person might begin with a hobby of scrapbooking and that expands to card making, origami, painting, woodworking, and beyond. That same person is often not limited to interests in crafts, but also loves to read, cook, and travel. With each new interest come more supplies. Since the previous interests were not completely abandoned, the items accumulate. She might have a few free hours on a weekend, and if the choice is pursuing a hobby or organizing the hobby, there is little internal debate to determine that organizing will have to wait until another day. Items purchased for a hobby that are not used are not discarded. These clients are extremely uncomfortable facing their feelings of guilt and regret over spending money on something and then never using it. Rather than face that feeling and what they believe it says about them, they tend to avoid and things continue to accumulate.

Struggling with time management is a fourth characteristic shared by many with CD and hoarding behaviors. They often start an activity only to realize hours later that they missed appointments or meals. This difficulty with time is also manifested in lacking a sense of how long something will take. They might look at a stack of the day's mail and believe it will take an hour, when in reality it takes them only 10 minutes at most. Overestimating how long an undesirable activity will take is a major disincentive to undertaking that activity.

A fifth CD characteristic is distractibility. Clients often report that they begin an organizing project only to find that they have been busy for a few hours with no visible results to show for their time and effort. A ringing phone, email alerts, a barking dog, and even the juggling of too many items they are trying to store in their working memories become distractions from which they are unable to recover. When trying to organize the accumulation of weeks of mail, a person with CD may find themselves getting stuck in reading a birthday card or deciding whether to attend a professional conference rather than grouping the mail into piles of recycling, shredding, filing, and action items.

Group members are given an overview of these common characteristics to facilitate their disclosure of how they experience these or other challenges. Future group sessions will continue to build on their understanding of what is happening in and around them that perpetuates the problem.

C. Homework

These three homework assignments are the same for all group sessions except for the last one. Sections two through six have additional assignments:

- Evaluate the group session
- Set a goal to be completed prior to the next session

Clutter-Image Rating Scale - Group members should be instructed that it is expected that most rooms will remain the same or even get worse if they are focusing their attention on one room. They will see little change if they try to make an impact in every area at once. This is often a difficult thing for some group members to accept – that consciously choosing to postpone some areas will get them to their goals faster. Once they adopt this plan, they will feel less overwhelmed and paralyzed, and changes will begin to occur.

D. Summary

The Fresh Start Group is typically attended by people who feel isolated and blamed for their chronic disorganization or hoarding. The first group session gives them a better understanding of how disorganized they are as well as a connection to others in similar situations. Group members are often happily surprised and hopeful when they see others who are further along in their recovery.

3

THE BRAIN'S ROLE: THINKING PATTERNS

A. Positive Reports and Review of Homework

At the start of sessions two through eight, group members are asked to share something that went well between the previous group and the current group.

The research shows that it is helpful in this group session to explain the rationale for stating aloud the positive things that happen.

With repetitive behaviors, thoughts, and feelings people are capable of creating state changes in the mind. Over time the mind teaches the brain to grow new neuro pathways, which allow thinking and acting to be done differently. The goal of behavioral change is the foundation of mental health. In order to effectively and infinitely change behaviors one must change the somatic state of the body. This minor technique of having members share what has gone well creates a positive somatic (feeling) state in the body. The members then receive external gratification from the support of other group members. They are challenged to recognize their strengths and accomplishments and receive positive feedback. These are some things that are often out of the reach for people who are chronically isolated. .

Homework is reviewed with an emphasis placed on the successes of each member. It is common for group members to express genuine excitement over the accomplishments of others. There is a natural understanding that even the smallest step toward becoming more organized can be a huge hurdle that was overcome. Group members who did not do the homework are asked to talk about the barriers they encountered and other members are invited to challenge and/or problem solve. For members who chose a too simple goal, good group dynamics will lead them to better homework outcomes in session three.

B. Cognitive Distortions

To get a general understanding the group reviews ten common cognitive distortions found below and on the Cognitive Distortions Overview in Part 2.5. Members who tend to be highly literal or perfectionistic often struggle with their need to fit examples neatly into one cognitive distortion or another. It can be difficult to handle the ambiguity of thoughts that can be examples of more than one cognitive distortion. Group members can be helped to recognize that the most important part is recognizing that a particular thought represents a cognitive distortion and then correcting it, rather than what name the distortion should be given. Examples are provided of how these are typically displayed by chronically disorganized and hoarding clients. Some of the examples used include:

1. *All-or-nothing thinking* – Clients often establish a goal that only serves to set them up for failure. They will often say "I need to organize my whole house this weekend" or "I will always follow the only-handle-it-once (OHIO) rule." What can happen when clients set out to follow the OHIO rule without exception, is that they run into an item about which they are not ready to decide. Instead of making an exception to the rule and creating a "to be decided' pile, they completely abandon their organizing efforts.

2. *Overgeneralization* - Statements like "I can never find anything" only serve to stop those with chronic disorganization and hoarding from discovering what works for them and then building off those strategies. Members who focus on the regrets they have about items they have thrown out or donated can see the fit with this cognitive distortion.

3. *Discounting positives* - "Why bother? When I am working on one area of my house, another gets messed up." We all feel this way at times. A more helpful thought includes recognition that there are periods of disorganization, and that maintenance is just another part of the process.

4. *Jumping to conclusions* - This distortion involves either mind reading or fortune telling. Commonly heard is a combination of both "I can spend hours organizing the kitchen and my husband will come home and say 'what about the bedroom?'"

5. *Should statements* - These have a way of generating the exact opposite of what the chronically disorganized and hoarding client expects. What they often do not realize is that these are value judgments that either make a person feel superior if they complete the "should", or feel worthless if they don't. Clients with chronic disorganization or hoarding often say things like "I should be more organized" or "I should be able to do this myself".

6. *Personalization* - A mother might assume she is to blame when her husband criticizes their child for not keeping her room neat.

7. Labeling – This involves assigning meaning or accepting the name calling of others; "I am a slob", instead of saying "I have developed sloppy behaviors."

8. *Emotional reasoning* – This is deciding truth by feeling states, and in our group it often takes the form of "I feel hopeless, so I must be hopeless."

9. *Magnifying or minimizing* – Group members often exaggerate or lessen the severity of how disorganized a room really is, although the latter is more prevalent with the hoarding population. When they live among substantial clutter and disorganization they can become anesthetized to the negative psychological and physical ramifications.

10. *Mental Filter* - When a person reports and thinks about the negatives, they overlook the positives and sometimes begin to believe that there are no positives. This is why we ask group members to voice something that went well for them during the week. Conversely, some clients will discount the negatives as a way to protect themselves from the overwhelming feelings they would likely experience if they saw their situation without the filter.

The group is led through an exercise[10] to help them identify their cognitive distortions and develop more helpful responses. On the front of an index card under the heading "Automatic Thought", members write an example of one automatic thought they had. Below that, under "Cognitive Distortion" they identify which cognitive distortions their thought represents. On the back of the card is the heading "Rational Response". After challenging their thinking and developing at least one rational response, they write it on the back of the index card. A sample of the index card can be found in Part 2.6.. Extra index cards are provided to make it easier for members to complete the homework related to this activity.

A. Negative Self-Talk

Each person typically demonstrates certain cognitive distortions and not others. These distortions become automatic ways of thinking and seeing the world. For those who are unable to overcome their faulty ways of thinking, life will be impacted negatively. They become a billboard for how they think; often an archetype of the worrier, the critic, the victim, or the perfectionist[11]. Following the discussion about cognitive distortions, group members are directed to think about the patterns of the things they automatically say to themselves. Group members who are new to cognitive-behavioral therapy (CBT) often have an easier time seeing themselves in one of the sub-personalities rather than critically examining their specific ways of thinking. Each is described and examples are given as described below:

1. *The Worrier* – These people often finds themselves asking "what if…?" followed by a negative expectation. They do not ask "what if I can pay my bills on time?" Instead they ask "what if I never pay my bills on time" Instead of the worry moving them to action, they become stuck in the worry. In group, members are challenged to allow themselves to answer their own "what if…?" questions. Fellow group members will offer perspective and help them problem-solve their way out of the worry.

2. *The Critic* – The self-talk of the critic is "I'm pathetic because I can't even keep one room uncluttered." This voice usually notices every flaw while ignoring or downplaying the accomplishments. The Critic compares the CD client to others, and in a belittling and negative fashion. The self-esteem of those with a critic style of self-talk cannot stand up to the constant and powerful criticism. Critics are helped to see that they judge with much more empathy and patience than they judge themselves.

3. *The Victim* – Their theme is one of hopelessness and helplessness. "This happened to me and there's no point in even trying." Sometimes they will express their beliefs that since they have had this problem so long they will just have to accept that they will have it forever. Depression is often the result of this thinking pattern. It is important to be wary that group members who enjoy the caretaking role do not further the belief that the victim is truly a victim.

4. *The Perfectionist* – Like the critic, the perfectionist holds herself to a higher standard than she does others. Unlike the critic, the motive of the perfectionist voice is not to belittle, but to motivate. She can become burned out by the need to have a perfectly organized home or donate to the "right" charity. Taking time during the assessment phase to either have a home visit or see pictures is extremely valuable when working with the perfectionist. It is not uncommon for someone to express interest in attending the group and present an image of themselves as a chronically disorganized individual living in a cluttered or hoarded home when, in reality, their perspective is skewed by perfectionism. The drive for perfection can be so paralyzing that clutter mounts because reaching the only acceptable outcome is overwhelming. Perfectionists often exude tremendous relief when someone else voices the belief that they are a perfectionist because their experience has been that no one can understand how that is possible when their home is cluttered, their bills are paid late, and they cannot find items they borrowed.

E. Effective Coping Tools

Identifying methods to cope and overcome the thinking patterns that influence chronic disorganization inevitably arise during the group discussion on these factors. At the end of the group there is time devoted exclusively to coping strategies. This is done so that group members leave with the message that there are ways to overcome cognitive challenges, and so that they have a simple reference list when they are trying to make changes in their own thinking.

F. Homework

The first three homework assignments are the same for all group sessions except for the last session:

- Evaluate the group session
- Set a goal to be completed prior to the next session
- Clutter-Image Rating Scale
- Section Homework
    - Cognitive distortions card - Group members are asked to choose at least one cognitive distortion that is different than the one chosen in group, and to complete the index card in a similar way. They are to write down any times when they were able to catch themselves using a cognitive distortion and what they did to correct it.
    - Negative self-talk – members are asked to record the negative self-talk they catch themselves using and what they did to correct it
    - Coping tools – members are asked to record their success with coping tools, including a new one they tried.
- Activity Homework – members are asked to each bring in an item from home that represents their struggle with disorganization, clutter or hoarding. See Chapter 1 for details. Additionally, group members are asked to anticipate and record how they would feel about letting the item go and what the outcome would be.

G. Summary

Those who suffer from chronic disorganization are typically struggling with feeling overwhelmed by their situations. By separating the components into the physical, emotional, and cognitive realms, the problem begins to seem manageable. Members begin to develop trust in each other as they discuss their cognitive challenges, and this trust will be needed in the next session when they bring in items from home and share their stories.

4

THE BRAIN'S ROLE: EXECUTIVE FUNCTIONS

A. Positive Reports and Review of Homework

At the start of sessions two through eight, group members are asked to share something that went well before the homework is reviewed.

Group members are asked to talk about the item they brought and how and why it was chosen. At this time they will also go over their activity homework responses. This discussion often becomes very emotional, especially for members who move out of their comfort zones and bring in items that are connected to a loss or troubled relationship. It has been our experience that people with chronic disorganization and hoarding are not lacking in empathy, compassion, and the ability to nurture others. This factor has the benefit of creating a group environment in which members share some of their most painful experiences and receive the care they need to let go of the past and items connected to it.

Occasionally there is a group member who misunderstood the assignment or regrets bringing in an item that they have no difficulty letting go. These members are given an opportunity to bring in a different item to the next group session, however it is still important to discuss the reasons they brought what they did. The opportunity to develop awareness that they avoid taking emotional risks or are not really ready to let things go should not be missed.

As members discuss their items, it is important to have them share the coping strategies they used to manage the emotions that arose in between the time the assignment was given and the start of this group session. Group members are not always aware of the healthy coping skills they use until they are asked to recollect and verbalize them. Sometimes members will discover that they are more capable of managing intense emotions than they believed.

The items that group members have brought to group can be set aside after the discussion and before the next portion of the group.

B. Weak or Overloaded Executive Functions

The group is given a brief education on the regions of the brain and the roles of each. They are taught that the term "executive function" refers to the brain's ability to pay attention, manage time and space, organize, categorize, plan, make decisions, inhibit impulses, and remember things. Some CD clients have poorly developed executive functions, and others have overloaded their working memories to the extent that their abilities to make decisions and remember things, for example, are compromised. The group time focuses on the following areas of information processing[12]:

1. *Attention* – Organizing and de-cluttering require focused mental energy on activities that are often unappealing and with which the person with chronic disorganization and hoarding are less skilled. Distractions must be minimized. Internal distractions, such as emotions, hunger, and thoughts must be battled along with external distractions such as phones ringing, dogs barking, and the visual stimulation of a cluttered environment. Those with ADHD are well aware of these challenges, along with their decreased abilities to overcome them to sustain attention to the task at hand. Attentional challenges include the ability to concentrate long enough to establish some type of process, attend to details, andsustain interest in order to complete what might be a tedious task. A common example is paperwork. The mail needs to be opened and decisions made about what needs to be acted upon, filed, or discarded. Then the action items will either need to be done immediately or a process must be established to ensure that they are completed. There must be a storage system in order to keep certain papers, and if none is already established,

the type needs to be decided upon and set up. Then the documents need to get into the proper places. The items to be discarded need to either be thrown out, recycled, or shredded. The levels of planning, detail, and persistence can be challenging even for those without ADHD.

2. *Planning and Problem-Solving* – Group members tend to either under- or over-estimate the need to plan their de-cluttering and organizing efforts. Those who underestimate will often start in the morning without having had anything to eat or drink. They have no trash bags, recycling containers, or boxes/bins contain groups of items. They quickly become frustrated or tired from having to stop what they are doing to retrieve basic supplies. The fatigue and frustration can turn into negative self-talk and feelings of hopelessness, so they quit and become depressed. Those group members who overestimate the need to plan will either feel overwhelmed at the thought of how to start or spend an excessive amount of time to create a perfect plan. In either case, the planning function impedes the work that needs to be done.

3. *Organization and Categorization* – The ability to create a reasonable number of categories is an essential skill for both organizing and de-cluttering. Research indicates that clients who hoard typically struggle categorizing their own items more than they do someone else's items[13], and we have found the same to be true for those with chronic disorganization who do not hoard. This may be due in part to the emotional attachment to their own things and what the things represent to them. Rather than seeing a collection of mugs, the chronically disorganized individual will see

some that they like when drinking tea, while others are for coffee. They see mugs they got as souvenirs on trips with their family, and others purchased to support a fellow artist at an arts festival.

4. *Decision-Making* – The ability to make decisions relies on a person's ability to weigh multiple options simultaneously, once again requiring attention skills. The personality styles discussed earlier play a major role here, not only because of the messages they give, but also because the messages themselves are a distraction. Decision making can easily be hampered by self-talk that asks "what if…?" or criticizes every decision made. In the mail example given earlier, it is easy to see how many decisions have to be made on everyday tasks that most of us complete with little awareness that we are even making decisions.

5. *Memory* – Many people leave out items to help them remember to complete a certain task; it could be a bill to pay, a purchase to return to a store, or a blouse to repair. The problem occurs when the tasks are not completed at a pace that keeps up with those items that are left out. Piles begin to form, and people have to shuffle through piles to find what they need. As the items churn and more time is spent trying to find where things were left, the belief that they need to leave things out to remember them becomes reinforced. Often there is no inherent memory problem, just a failure with relying on a system of visual cues coupled with a lack of task completion.

F. Strategies to Improve Executive Functioning

The group is given a brief list of ideas that can help with executive functioning deficits, and they are asked to contribute other strategies that work for them. This is another opportunity for group members to feel helpful and competent. Seeing themselves this way can carry over into their functioning outside of the group in decreasing the paralysis that often comes with feeling incompetent.

G. Homework

The first three homework assignments are the same for all group sessions except for the last one:

- Evaluate the group session
- Set a goal to be completed prior to the next session
- Clutter-Image Rating Scale
- Section homework
  - Executive Functions – members are asked to think about and record how they think their lives would be different if they had improvement in their executive functions and which strategies they tried were the most effective.
- Activity Homework- Before the homework is given at the end of this session, group members should be reminded that if they choose to leave them, their items will be locked and kept safe. They are then asked to decide whether to leave them with the group leaders until the next week or to take them home. If they leave the items, they do not need to make a permanent decision until group eight. The homework for the last group was for group members to anticipate how they would feel about letting an item go and what the outcome would be. The assignment for this week

is to record how they actually felt and what actually happened as a result. The purpose is to illustrate that expectations are often worse than reality. Additionally, they are asked to consider what they want to happen to the items they left at group.

H. Summary

The Fresh Start session on executive functions decreases blame and instead helps group members look at causes of and solutions to their situations. They also begin to see some of the positive aspects to the way their brains function.

5

THE BRAIN'S ROLE: OTHER COGNITIVE FACTORS

A. Positive Reports and Review of Homework

At the start of sessions two through eight, group members are asked to share something that went well.

Homework is reviewed, with attention given to the differences group members report in their anticipated feelings and outcomes and actual feelings and outcomes. Most members will quickly recognize their tendencies to believe letting go of things will be worse than it actually is. Often there are group members who will share their continued regrets for letting go of something years ago. It is important to discuss that the regretted decisions are few, and they forget about many things of which they let go that they did not regret. It is equally important that group members understand that they will continue to make some decisions they regret; the only way to avoid that is to make no decisions at all. This understanding can be a needed perspective and fits well with the cognitive distortions topic. Extra time can be taken to process the emotions and thoughts about the regrets that group members experience.

B. Other Cognitive Factors

Elaborative processing[14]

Group members are generally unfamiliar with this term, which refers to the creative ability to generate an endless number of possible uses for an item or way to do something. Prior to describing what this is, the group engages in an activity to illustrate it. A simple bottle cap is set in front of the group and they are given sixty seconds to each write down as many uses as they can think of. At the end of the sixty seconds, they are asked how many they wrote. The person with the most then reads her list, with other members then only reading a use no one else named. This activity provides an excellent opportunity to not only understand elaborative processing and how it is a problem, but also how some members can become paralyzed. Often there is at least one group member who can only come up with a handful of ideas, and it is important to discuss their experiences. Time pressure, competition, perfectionism, and confusion are common causes.

In real life situations, in order to decide what to do with an unwanted item or set up a filing system, for example, one must limit the options available to her. The chronically disorganized or hoarding individual has an amazing gift of being able to imagine an infinite number of possibilities. They easily imagine creative uses for things others determine to be useless and ways to set up the filing system of their dreams. While the ideas themselves are not a problem, following them through to completion is. It is noble to want to connect old blankets to the humane society, but if the nearest location is 50 miles in the opposite direction they typically travel, it is unlikely to happen.

Beliefs about usefulness, waste, and responsibility[15]

Group members often assume an unreasonable sense of their own responsibilities to items and the world. If an item still has use to someone it "should" not be discarded. Even a bottle of lotion that is nearly empty and they have no intention to use, must be kept in case they or someone else needs it. This sense of responsibility lacks a plan to fulfill good intentions, and so then becomes a problem for the person with chronic disorganization or hoarding. The group members typically share their guilt about how many gifts they have for people that they have never given and other items they struggle to discard because they still have use. Often members connect each other to local resources that help them get those items to people in need.

Beliefs about identity[16]

In an ideal situation, group members who see themselves as thrifty, for example, might only buy needed items on sale and then use what they already have before purchasing more. For those with chronic disorganization and hoarding however, the struggle occurs when they buy things solely because they were good deals. They maintain their belief in their identity as thrifty despite the reality that they end up throwing out expired items, having to donate other useful items to make room for the new "deals", and purchase duplicates because they can't find the originals. Sometimes the identity issues are reflected in attachment to items as if the identity would vanish in the absence of the item. Group members who are retired teachers often struggle to let go of gifts and notes from students, their work wardrobe, and even bulletin board items. Group members challenge each other to focus on both being able to have the identity without the items and forging new identities moving forward.

Procrastination

Surely everyone has procrastinated more than once. For those with chronic disorganization and hoarding, procrastination gets played out through their subpersonalities. For the victims, it is a way of life and can't be helped, while the worrier becomes consumed with worry about it, yet does not change this behavior. The mantra of the critic is "you are just lazy". The perfectionist sometimes uses procrastination as a way to manage the perfectionism, convincing themselves that they did well considering the limited amount of time they spent on the task.

The causes of procrastination are broken down into three categories (see below), and group members are asked to begin to think about their own procrastination. When the broad term "procrastination" is looked at from the perspective of multiple causes it begins to be seen as something that can be changed.

1. Causes that are related to feelings/moods, including:
    a. The task is unpleasant
    b. You feel overwhelmed
    c. You are not in the mood
    d. You don't want the responsibility
    e. You fear success

   f. You "thrive" on the adrenalin rush caused by waiting until the last minute

2. Causes that are related to thoughts/cognitions, including:
   a. The task is too difficult
   b. The goals are unclear
   c. It seems unimportant
   d. It might go away
   e. You need time to mull it over

3. Causes that are related to behaviors/practicalities, including:
   a. Interruptions
   b. Disorganization
   c. A lack of information
   d. Not enough time
   e. It isn't due for a while
   f. You want to do it perfectly

The procrastination handout found in Part 2.9 is given to group members and includes at least one strategy that can be used to battle each cause of procrastination.

D. Strategies for Cognitive Factors

The group is given a brief list of ideas that can help with the cognitive factors identified in this group session. The downward arrow technique is reviewed in greater detail, and members are given the Downward Arrow worksheet, found in Part 2.10. They are asked to contribute other strategies that work for them.

E. Homework

The first three homework assignments are the same for all group sessions except for the last one:

- Evaluate the group session
- Set a goal to be completed prior to the next session
- Clutter-Image Rating Scale
- Section homework
    - Other Cognitive Factors – members are asked to think about and record how they think elaborative processing; beliefs about usefulness, waste, and responsibility; beliefs about identity; and procrastination affect them. They are also asked to try a new strategy for overcoming these challenges and record the result.

F. Summary

This session completes the cognitive portion of the Fresh Start program. The process of becoming more organized in the physical world begins with organizing one's thoughts and feelings. Cognitive factors span three group sessions because of the amount of content and amount of discussion it generates. Although most of our group members have some experience with therapy, they have not always been given the knowledge-base to think about their thinking habits and the skills to change those unhelpful thoughts. They discover factors that contribute to their disorganization and begin to take control over some of these.

6

EMOTIONAL AND PHYSICAL FACTORS

A. Positive Reports and Review of Homework

At the start of sessions two through eight, group members are asked to share something that went well.

B. Acquiring

Because "stuff" impacts almost all of those who attend the group, we provide a framework for thinking about how that stuff enters our homes. Clients readily understand the active forms of acquiring: on-line, in store, and picking up items given away by others. Less realized are the passive forms of acquiring, such as reading a brochure in a doctor's office and then taking the brochure home. Group members are typically unaware of the ways they passively acquire: parents die and they inherit items, junk mail, or a flyer is on their car windshield and it makes its way into their homes. Types of acquiring can be understood by looking at the figure below. The x axis represents outcomes, with the upper quadrants representing those times when we intend to acquire (we have a need to meet), and the lower quadrants representing those times when we do not intend to acquire anything (no needs to meet). The y axis represents the intention. Group members are asked to be more aware of the times they are in each of the four quadrants. When they are seeking, they should examine their intentions to be sure that what they are seeking satisfies some criteria.

Group members should examine the outcomes they experience. When they are not acquiring is it because they feel content with what they have, are working on stopping the acquiring at least until they can de-clutter or get organized, or because they are actively turning down potential acquisitions? They should be mindful of the good choices they are making and celebrate those successes with others in the group.

Members are given a small card they can carry with them to help evaluate whether or not they should acquire a particular item. On one side this card asks questions to help them decide whether or not to acquire something. On the opposite side of the card are similar questions designed to help them when deciding whether or not to get rid of something. Information about purchasing coated or laminated cards can be found in Appendix B.

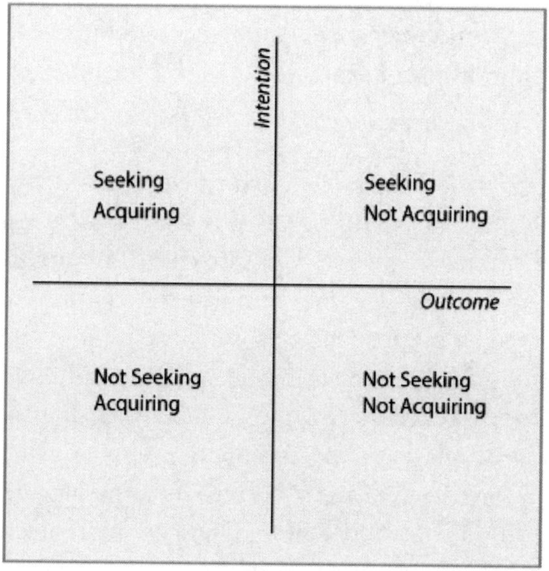
Intention
Seeking
Acquiring
Seeking
Not Acquiring
Outcome
Not Seeking
Acquiring
Not Seeking
Not Acquiring

C. Common Emotional Factors

It is very important for group members to understand the various emotional factors that impact chronic disorganization and hoarding. What we most often see are factors related to unresolved traumatic experiences, depression insufficiently treated, and a number of anxiety related disorders. Although, clinicians are aware that trauma, depression and anxiety have strong physical components, for the purposes of educating group members we found it works better to discuss these issues under the description of Emotional Factors.

There is a sense of relief when members learn, for example, that the fatigue, hopelessness, lack of energy, and indecisiveness they experience may be due to untreated major depressive disorder, and that those symptoms can be both cause and effect of chronic disorganization and hoarding. Some studies indicate that as high as 75% of people with hoarding disorder have experienced a comorbid mood disorder. Some of the most common co-occurring emotional challenges are listed for group members, and they are encouraged to add to the list any they believe also impact chronic disorganization and hoarding and to process their experiences.

In addition to mood disorders such as depression, a person may be experiencing troubling affective states as a result of unprocessed traumatic events. A phrase coined by the EMDR community is "big T's,(Trauma) and little t's (trauma)". A big trauma refers to an event such as 911. A little trauma might be that you left your cell phone at home, and you did not notice until you arrived at work. No one goes through life without trauma. How people view the traumatic events and the relationship they have to their inner coping styles may be descriptive and aid in diagnostic profiles. There are many factors to consider when assessing why and how much of the traumatic experience will cause unpleasant symptoms or even be psychiatrically diagnosed. Some human beings are hard-wired to handle and process traumatic events in an asymptomatic manner. Their autonomic nervous systems seems to have the capability to regulate between sympathetic and parasympathic, without much interference in functioning. Others experience more regulation difficulties, and their fight, flight, freeze systems of the sympathetic nervous system are activated quicker and more often. In addition to having intrinsic trauma shields or not, people perceive traumatic events in different ways. This may be because of internal processing, external learning or a combination of both. If your client reported at their intake assessment that they were involved in, or had a strong reaction to, a traumatic event, you will want to further assess how or if they have been treated. Trauma that is unprocessed (untreated) is stored in the body and can manifest as other physical and or emotional factors.

D. Common Physical Factors

Often overlooked is the impact that physical factors have on chronic disorganization and hoarding. The group members' self-blame that leads to hopelessness and inactivity is addressed as they get an understanding of the interplay between their physical pain and low energy and chronic disorganization and hoarding. Many people who struggle with chronic disorganization and hoarding have physical conditions that impact their abilities to keep up with the daily demands of a household. According to the National Alliance on Mental Illness (NAMI), people who hoard are three times as likely to be obese or overweight. Many people are not able to climb over the barrier of clutter to access the refrigerator or stove in order to prepare healthy meals. Instead, they opt to eat out due to this accessibility issue. They are more likely to choose fast foods because they are less expensive than a sit down restaurant meal and they can use a drive through option. The drive through option further increases their social isolation and decreases their need for good personal hygiene. It takes energy and an absence of pain to be able to bring in and attend to the mail, put away groceries, wash dishes, return things from one floor of a home to another, and take out the trash. Because most of us take these abilities for granted, group members feel guilty and ashamed that they cannot, and they do not grant themselves the same compassion they do to others. The negative feelings about themselves lead to further inactivity rather than a search for options to ameliorate the situation, such as hiring in-home help. Some of the most common co-occurring physical challenges are listed for group members, including chronic pain, arthritis, fatigue, fibromyalgia, visual impairment, obesity, other chronic illnesses, and HALT, the acronym for…

Hungry
Angry
Lonely
Tired

…so they can keep in mind the basic factors they need to take care of in order to be able to address the chronic disorganization and hoarding behaviors. They are encouraged to add to the list any they believe also impact chronic disorganization and hoarding, and to address these underlying physical conditions.

E. Self-Soothing Tools

As group members begin to have intellectual understandings of causes and effects of chronic disorganization and hoarding, they are challenged to give themselves the same compassion and empathy that they give to each other. As the shame and blame start to lessen, group members are eager for tools to manage the emotions and physical challenges they encounter. This portion of the group is critical for empowering group members to take action and believe they can manage the strong emotions that inevitably arise. The group handout includes a list of self-soothing tools, ranging from those they can easily do (e.g. listening to music), to those that may require additional education or training (e.g. hypnotherapy). Creative thinking is encouraged so that members can add to the list anything they find helpful.

F. Homework

The first three homework assignments are the same for all group sessions except for the last one:

- Evaluate the group session
- Set a goal to be completed prior to the next session
- Clutter-Image Rating Scale
- Section homework
    - Acquiring – members are asked to recall if they were able to resist acquiring and to describe the situation
    - Self-Soothing – members are instructed to try a new self-soothing tool and to record the result

G. Summary

This session helps members see their chronic disorganization and hoarding in a larger context. They learn the cause and effect relationship between acquiring and disorganization and emotional and physical factors. Group members typically begin to bond over their shared struggles and benefit from the compassion and interest shown by others in the group.

7

THE INFLUENCE OF PERSONALITY TYPE: DISC MODEL

A. Positive reports and review of homework

At the start of sessions two through eight, group members are asked to share something that went well.

B. DISC Model

The DISC is a behavioral assessment tool based on the theory of William Marston, PhD, that there are four basic personality types: Dominance, Inducement, Submission, and Compliance. According to Marston's theory, people demonstrate their emotions through these personality types. The types are based on a person's perception of his control over the environment and his environment[17], as shown in the table below:

	Belief in Own Ability to Control the Environment	Belief in the Favorability of the Environment
Dominance	Yes	No
Inducement	Yes	Yes
Submission	No	Yes
Compliance	No	No

William Clark turned Marston's theory into an assessment, and there have since been many adaptations of the names given to the four personality types, but each always beginning with the letters D-I-S-C. In the Fresh Start group we typically use Driver/Director, Influencer, Steady/Supporter, and Cautious/Contemplator.

It is helpful to have group members begin their DISC assessments as they arrive, rather than waiting for all members before starting. This gives more time for people to ask questions and have it completed without taking up too much group time. The self-assessment tool we use can be found in 2.13 of this manual, but other versions can also be used. The assessment is done in group rather than as homework so that no members are waiting for others who may not have completed it for homework.

Some group members are aware of the model and have taken test in work environments; but for those who are not familiar, a brief overview is given. The names and descriptions of the four behavior types are not shared until after the completion of the assessment tool as a way to minimize influencing the test taking. Group members who have wireless devices can access the tool in our group box.com folder and their results will be automatically tallied. After all group members have their primary styles indicated by the tool, full descriptions of each are given, and three handouts are given:

1. DISC Quadrant Model (found in Part 2.14)
2. DISC Traits (found in Part 2.15)
3. DISC Communication Strategies (found in Part 2.16)

The DISC Communication Strategies handout is provided as an additional resource to help group members communicate with other personality types and to better understand the types of communication habits they need from others.

Members are encouraged to react to the rating of their primary styles, and to discuss the pros and cons they experience. It is important for them to understand that no one is always and completely operating out of one quadrant. The healthy personality adapts to situations and the people around them, and has one primary style that serves as the default behavior.

Group members can apply what they learn about their DISC styles to their typical de-cluttering and organizing habits. The Drivers/Directors are rarely seen in our groups because they are the "Get it Done" types who like immediate results and are not averse to conflict. These traits tend to be inconsistent with chronic disorganization and hoarding.

Influencers are among the most commonly seen in our groups. These "Get it Out There" types see the world as full of possibilities and options, and they dislike paperwork and details. It is easy to see how acquiring occurs when everything represents something to which they can add their creative touch. Organizing can easily become an avoided task of details. Influencers can benefit from an understanding that they are often motivated by recognition and freedom of expression. If they are going to ask for help from others, they will work best with people with high energy, who do not believe there is one "right" way to do things, and who will minimize chaos.

The Steady/Supporter personality types can find themselves in chronic disorganization and hoarding in part because of their avoidance of change. Letting go of things represents a change, and if items have been kept because of emotional attachments, it can be even more challenging. These "Get Along" types can benefit by getting help because of their affinity for cooperative relationships. Choosing a person who makes sudden changes or tends toward aggressive confrontation is destined to fail.

Cautious/Contemplator types are often found in our groups, although at first glance this seems counter-intuitive. One would think that their comfort in details, rules, and systems would lend themselves to organization, but it is just these traits that create problems. These "Get it Right" types can become lost in details and their perfectionism leads them to give up. They can become lost in decision-making and creating perfect systems. If they are going to get help, they will respond best to someone who knows the "rules" that apply, but also can be patient enough to allow the Cautious/Contemplator individual to come to a decision when there are competing rules.

D. Homework

The first two homework assignments are the same for all group sessions except for the last one:

- Evaluate the group session
- Set a goal to be completed prior to the next session
- Clutter-Image Rating Scale
- Section Homework –
    - DISC - Because sections 6 and 7 are intellectually heavy and there is much to absorb, the only section homework is to write down any lingering questions or insights about the model
- Activity Homework - members are asked to each bring in an item from home that represents their struggle with disorganization, clutter or hoarding. See Chapter 1 for details. Additionally, group members are asked to anticipate and record on the Activity Homework Page how they would feel about letting the item go and what the outcome would be.

E. Summary

Sessions on understanding the influences of personality types are designed to help members better understand themselves in ways that are without value judgment. Instead of looking at what is wrong with them, they look at how to take advantage of their natural tendencies.

8

THE INFLUENCE OF PERSONALITY TYPE: MYERS-BRIGGS TYPE INDICATOR®

FASCOPY
FASCOPY

A. Positive reports and review of homework

At the start of sessions two through eight, group members are asked to share something that went well.

B. Myers-Briggs

According to the Myers & Briggs Foundation, The Myers-Briggs Type Indicator® (MBTI®) is designed to bring practical usefulness to the psychological types described by C.G. Jung.[18] The basic theory is that while human behavior often seems random, there is actually great consistency among people in the ways they perceive and interpret. The research of Isabel Briggs-Myers and Katherine Briggs led to the identification of four preferences and 16 distinct personality types. The four preferences leading to 16 possible preferences are:

- A person's focus of energy and locus of control is either Extroversion (E) or Introversion (I)
- Gathering information and the focus of attention is either Sensing(S) or Intuition (N)
- Sorting information and ways of deciding is either Thinking (T) or Feeling (F)
- Acting on information and interacting with the environment is either Judging (J) or Perceiving (P)

The format of the group does not lend itself to administering the MBTI® to attendees. Instead, the group is given a quick overview of the Myers-Briggs theory and each of the four preferences. Members are asked to select those preferences that seem to fit the most for them, and they come up with their four-letter personality type. Many in the group have taken the MBTI® at some point, and most have at least a beginning understanding of the instrument and its purposes.

Group discussion is focused on the ways in which knowing more about oneself can lead to success both in intra- and interpersonally. In terms of their chronic disorganization and hoarding, group members are given ways to use their strengths and overcome weaknesses, such as:

- Extroverts can get help from others and talk through a strategy
- Introverts can take a limited amount of reflection time before making a decision
- Sensing types can either gather a limited number of facts or gather facts for a limited amount of time to better understand a problem. They can also give themselves a deadline for using something or else it gets discarded.
- Intuitive types can vary their strategies to keep it interesting, or de-clutter/organize based on what inspires them on a given day
- Thinkers can use pro and con lists and decide based on what is most "fair" to the objects in question
- Feelers can focus on what is best for their family and giving to needy people and causes
- Judging types can work off a small list that includes "play" time
- Perceptive types can work in small time segments, finding ways to make routine tasks fun

C. Homework

The first three homework assignments are the same for all group sessions except for the last one:

- Evaluate the group session
- Set a goal to be completed prior to the next session
- Clutter-Image Rating Scale
- Section Homework –
    - Myers-Briggs - Because sessions 6 and 7 are intellectually heavy and there is much to absorb, the only section homework is to write down any lingering questions or insights about the model

- Activity Homework - the homework for the last group was for group members to anticipate how they would feel about letting an item go and what the outcome would be. The assignment for this week is to record how they actually felt and what actually happened as a result. The purpose is to illustrate that expectations are often worse than reality. Additionally, they are asked to consider what they want to happen to the items they left at group.
- Wellness Plan – When the wellness plan forms (found in Part 2.2) are distributed, group members are asked to complete items 1a through 1l. This will involve them reviewing their handouts from previous group sections, and considering whether they have additional questions or additions that need to be addressed in order for them to move forward. Group members should also look at items 2 through 5 so they can be prepared to address those in the final group session. The Wellness Plan serves as a way for group members to address any questions or issues they have with any of the section content. It also gives them an important reference tool to use in the future.

D. Summary

Sessions that focus on understanding the influences of personality types are designed to help members better understand themselves in ways that are without value judgment. Instead of looking at what is wrong with them, they look how to take advantage of their natural tendencies.

9

MOVING FORWARD

A. Positive Reports and Review of Homework

At the start of sessions two through eight, group members are asked to share something that went well.

Homework is briefly reviewed.

Group members are asked to make final decisions about each of the items they brought. They can take one or both items to keep, give away, or destroy; or they can have one or both items donated or destroyed by the group leaders. It has been our experience that group members almost always ask that their items be donated by the group leaders. There are occasions when someone chooses to keep an item, and that decision should be supported. The goal of the group is not for members to feel pressured to get rid of things. The goal is for them to get better about making decisions about their stuff that support their goals and values. When they feel supported in their decisions to keep items, group members are often empowered to get rid of other things. They begin to look inside themselves for answers and trust their abilities to know what is right for them.

B. Wellness Planning

The group members are asked to go over their lingering questions and issues from all of the prior group sessions, as outlined in the Wellness Plan item number 1. Not only is this the opportunity for group members to further their progress, but it is also an opportunity to evaluate the group content and process. If there are areas in which several group members are really struggling, it could mean that the delivery of the content needs to be modified or that more time is needed to process those issues.

After item number one is completed, the group will move on to address their stress awareness and management skills. This portion of the Wellness Plan reminds them to expect stress moving forward, and that they have the knowledge and skills to be able to cope with what comes their way.

Concrete planning finishes the plan. Group members will leave the group with plans to continue moving forward to tackle their de-cluttering and organizing goals.

C. Group Feedback

Group members are asked to share with one or more group members something they learned from that person specifically and something they believe is a growth area for that person specifically. They can choose one person or two different people for each feedback item. This activity reinforces the increased abilities group members have to give and receive feedback. Group members are often surprised and delighted to discover that one of their peers learned something from them. Discussing growth areas underscores the fact that change is an ongoing process. The phrase "growth area" helps remove the stigma associated with chronic disorganization and hoarding.

D. Self-Hypnosis

The group is told that they will be learning a technique of self-hypnosis. After a description of what will occur and the pros and cons are discussed, group members are given the choice whether to participate. Anyone not participating has the option of sitting quietly in the room with their eyes open or going to the waiting room until the end of the activity. This is one technique that, when practiced, can relieve the anxiety that is contributing to difficulty making decisions about stuff.

Hypnotherapy is a combination of teaching self-hypnosis and an ongoing therapeutic relationship for support, symptom reduction, and somatic education. The hypnotic state is a natural state of being for animals and humans. There are 5 levels of consciousness. The following are ways that may be applied to understanding the levels as they could be adopted to clearing clutter.

1. Alert - You are clearing a room
2. Light Trance Daydreaming - You are idly thinking about clearing a room
3. Moderate Trance - You are imagining yourself in the room clearing it
4. Deep Trance - You physically feel yourself moving, lifting, and sorting your stuff
5. Sleep - You dream of being involved in clearing the room

A point to recognize is that once the subconscious mind accepts an idea, it begins to execute that idea. Day dreaming is a form of a hypnotic state of mind. A person is not asleep, rather operating out of a dual awareness. We operate daily using 90% of our subconscious mind and only 10% of our conscious mind. To teach the person self-hypnosis, have them sit in a comfortable position, not lying down. Group members are instructed to begin by taking three deep breaths, letting each muscle group begin to feel like wet noodles, collapsing. Next, they are to focus attention on an area in the room - a picture, window, or spot on the wall and hold their gazes there. Then they are told that their eyelids are becoming heavy and their eyelashes are sticking together like glue. The leader recites something similar to:

"I am going to count from 10 all the way down, down, down to one. 10…9…8…7…6…5…4…3…2…1 Clear your mind of any thoughts. When your mind wanders just gently bring it back. Concentrate on your breath; effortlessly going in and out; round and round. Just allow the rhythm of breath to allow you to go deeper into relaxation."

Once they are in a room in their minds' eyes, the leader can instruct them to visualize clearing one portion of a room of their choice. The more specific the leader's instructions are to use all five senses, the more useful the hypnotic trance will be. To bring them back: just take three deep cleansing breaths as you count from one all the way up to 10. At 10 have them slowly come back into the room. They are instructed to notice their surroundings, wiggle their muscles, and breathe normally.

When the exercise is concluded there is a short debriefing where group members are gently asked: "How did you do?" This gives them ownership of their individual processes in addition to fostering group feedback.

Most of our group participants have not trained their minds and bodies to enjoy the deep sense of comfort that a self-hypnotic state can bring. They are living in perpetual states of anxiety and indecision, never getting off auto pilot. This can manifest in increased anxiety, depression or anger when challenged to part with belongings.

F. Summary

The section on emotional and physical factors is a time of reflection, clarification, and celebration. There is often a mixture of hopefulness and anxiety about the future. Group members typically discuss with each other the possibility of getting together to continue to give and receive support and encouragement.

G. Tips for running this group session

- If the group does not have a leader trained in hypnotherapy, various relaxation and guided imagery techniques can be used.

- We encourage group members to bring recording devices if they want to record the process in order to practice at home.
- The group members may give all their feedback to certain members, such as those that had bigger breakthroughs or who are more receptive to hearing the growth areas. It is important to ensure that after gives their feedback, that no members have been left out of hearing from their peers. The group leaders can ask for a member to volunteer to share something they learned from the member(s) who have not yet heard that and or the group leaders can give their response. The same holds true for the growth area feedback.
- When closing out the group, the members are told that if they need additional resources or referrals they can contact either group leader.

10

SESSION EVALUATIONS AND OUTCOMES

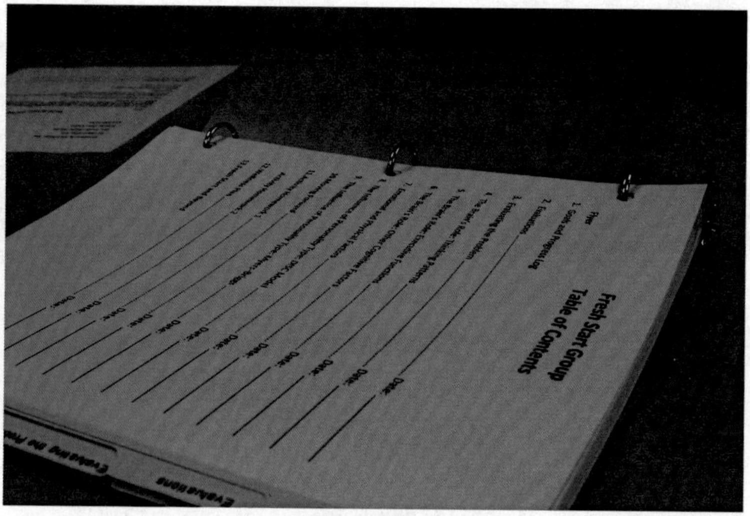
Fresh Start Group
Table of Contents

Session Evaluations

As described earlier, in the handouts for each Fresh Start group session members are asked to record their thoughts and feelings about the best and worst things about that group session. We use this feedback to help us shape the format, structure, and content of future groups. Additionally, the responses to these questions have provided valuable diagnostic information on group members that helps us shape their treatment plans outside of the group process.

Format and Structure

When we ran the first group, there were numerous group members that provided feedback on the "worst thing" such as:

- "A little too dark - increase sense of depression; font too small to read well"
- "Lack of a table"
- "Too hot"

Based on these comments, we changed the room we used. This change clearly had a positive effect on at least one group member who, the very next week, responded that her "best thing" was:

> "I can't say enough about how much BETTER tonight's environment is from previous weeks! The room is well-ventilated, roomy with comfy chairs. Good mix of warm incandescent light and full spectrum light to write by (having the desk surface to write on is so great)."

As group leaders, we can become so focused on the content and process of the group, that we forget how the physical surroundings profoundly impact some people, particularly those with sensory issues.

Another common "worst thing' theme we read on evaluations was about the length of the group. Some examples were:

- "Not enough time to process info"
- "Not enough time - too short; would like to have an additional half hour to share experiences with our group members"
- "Not long enough - could have gone on at least 1 hour longer"
- "As usual the time went very quickly"
- "Too short concepts too big"

The first group we ran was four weeks, so we made the next group five weeks. When we continued to receive the same feedback, we made the following group six weeks. The comments of the "worst thing" did not change, so we added two weeks to get to our present length of eight weeks. While group members talk about feeling sad that their group experience is ending, the "not enough time" comments have drastically reduced. In addition, we started a monthly, optional follow-up group called Fresh Start and Beyond. That will be described in Chapter 11. The following are some of the "best thing" feedback we received about the structure and format of the group:

- "Hearing everyone's growth"
- "Listening to other people about their situation and how you can draw some similarities and add some suggestions that might help."
- "I truly appreciate Joey's flexibility to allow us to go off the outline and share our stories and traumas"
- "Karen's presentation with visual board"
- "Listening and learning"
- "Time to process and talk about personal struggle"
- "Nice job setting a controlled environment where people feel free to share. Personal authenticity of teacher is helpful in setting people at ease. Perfect size group"
- "Going over everything brings it up and makes it clear in my mind."
- "Joey's efforts to keep each of us from elaborating off topic. Keeping us on task will take a firm hand"
- "Being given this nice neat organized notebook"
- "Lots of info and good handouts"
- "Flags for homework"
- "Personalized attention with question and answer period since I unfortunately missed last week's session"

- "Small group size allowed for more sharing. Got to know other members"
- "Asking each of us to reveal ourselves however we felt comfortable - no rules about what to say/what to include. Very comfortable approach"

While we did not make changes based on these comments, they confirmed our belief in the value of the group process and some of the ways we chose to structure and shape the program.

Content

We strongly encourage group members to tell us the truth about their group experiences so we can continue to make the group better. Some group members need a few weeks before they feel confident that what they say will not be held against them in the weeks that follow. Content is often an area in which group members tend to feel safest sharing their opinions. It seems that for every person whose "best thing" is cognitive distortions or Myers-Briggs, there is another member for whom it was the "worst thing". As such, we did not include those comments below. We continue to look for ways to make split-opinion topics such as those more beneficial for everyone, and we recognize that not everyone will be happy with everything we do in the Fresh Start Group.

Below are some of the "best thing" comments about the content that were not about the major topics on the agendas and/or things that just came up during the group discussions:

- "I liked discussing how to deal with triggers"
- "Finding out that trauma causes triggers"
- "Coping tools"
- "Hearing success stories and writing goals"
- "Using STOP and asking questions how I will use it"
- "Learning the 3 P's of stress management"

- "Info on how the brain works"
- "Processing potential of getting rid of stuff"
- "Learning possible causes"
- "Getting to leave something here and making a bit more room"
- "Rating the severity of the thought - what can you do to challenge it (replacement phrases) [and] SUDS - subjective units of distress"
- "Clarifying the problems, individual photos of rooms"
- "Hearing that "we" are not bad people…just "broken" to some extent (perhaps from the past)"

The "worst thing" comments related to the content of the Fresh Start group were:

- "Fight/flight/freeze info"
- "I have not been able to figure out the point of this course. There are too many big concepts. Is the point of this course to de stress and learn those techniques so that we don't hoard or clutter? Think course should be 6-8 weeks."
- "Didn't know what to bring in for hw…. So much info overwhelming"
- "Hole metaphor - how depressing"
- "Too much time waiting for people to arrive, doing bookwork, setting up, etc. When someone is paying for a class he/she expects it to start on time (sorry late people) and be loaded with info for the allotted time… Ideally [group members] would come to class knowing their personality type tendency and the teacher could explain how they relate to hoarding and "knowing thyself" would help in the de-hoarding process."

As we discussed earlier, we changed the number of group sessions to address the comments about the Fresh Start being too short. The "worst thing" comments above were very helpful because it told us that one of the important reasons group members thought Fresh Start needed to be longer was because they felt overwhelmed. At least one member clearly articulated that there was too much content for them to absorb in such a short period of time. Expanding to eight weeks addressed this.

In the "worst thing" comments above are words such as "class", "teacher", and "course". Since this is a psychotherapy group and not a class, we realized that we needed to first, make sure that potential group members were clear about the differences between the two. Second, we needed to start the first group session with reminders about the expectations of being in a psychotherapy group and that the group process is likely to stir up intense emotions. Third, we learned that group members will often reveal important clinical information about themselves when giving feedback about the group. We addressed the last bullet point comment above by explaining why we sometimes have people complete forms in the group, to discuss reasonable accommodations for those whose reasons for being in the group (ADD, hoarding, depression) might be the reasons for arriving late, and to build compassion for others.

Intrapersonal

Often in group there are members who speak infrequently and share less of their stories and emotions than do most group members. It is easy to infer that they are shy or not engaged in the group. The following "best thing" session evaluation comments indicate that members are often processing intense emotions when they are silent.

- "Seeing and admitting how much I've done and grieving how my health may be attributed to trauma, has been involved with my organization"
- "Realizing what I have done positive"
- "Identifying with others: I too am a relentless researcher. I took the Flylady approach - I am creative!! I am deep!! I am sidetracked!!"
- "Chance to feel like I could express the pain that goes with the chaos"
- "The aha! moment of recognizing the perfectionist in myself. I have never really viewed myself in that way yet it explains some of my anxiety and frustrations"
- "Talking through struggles I have. Arriving on time"

Group members found some intrapersonal experiences to be their "worst thing":

- "Although I gained insight, I haven't seen much shift (yet has been able to give myself recognition) from who I was when I started the class"
- "My own emotional reaction to what people were talking about"
- "Hard to be only one with serious mental illness diagnosis"
- "Bringing up the feelings makes me sad"
- "Being angry at my parents. I talked way too much"
- "I wasn't totally there today-felt disoriented"
- "Knowing some things about myself"
- "It's the first group session that I wanted to end, that triggered some sadness, anger, fear? Not sure what, that I don't want to uncover and have erupt. But I don't remember exactly what was being said when I had that sensation."
- "It brought up some things about my mom and gifts and the watch brought up the thought of my broken

jewelry boxes. Also, I feel like I took the easy way out with the stuff I brought in."

- "Not being able to "fix" others problems"
- "The sense that I wasn't changing fast enough. That is a "me" thing though, not a group thing."
- "Realizing I probably have a much longer way to go than I originally thought"
- "Can't articulate my feeling but I know I was restless for some reason"

It is fascinating that what members identify as the "worst thing", as psychotherapists we see as positive. We view the self-knowledge and ability to experience emotions as signs of growth and change. We use this information to help group members understand what they are experiencing and how they are judging their feelings as bad, rather than just being aware of them. When possible, we further discuss and process these comments in individual sessions. When the group members are working with different therapists and we have signed consents to release information, we pass the session evaluations on to the clients' therapists.

Interpersonal

Some of the most inspiring "best thing" comments are connected to the relationships group members develop with each other.

- "Comfortable with group and Karen. Lots of discussion - making us think about who and why we are doing the things we do."
- "Good group interaction"
- "That I am not alone in this situation"
- "Wisdom of the group"
- "Sharing of our stories"

- "Good mix of people - great that you've worked with each of us and can give us feedback when we're on or off track"
- "Hearing others admit issues/validate my issues and experiences"
- "Knowing that I am not alone "no judgment" thing great"
- "Seeing how brave [Joyce] was"
- "Following each member's explanation of 'brought' item"
- "Nancy complimented me"
- "Encouragement from all. Karen's encouragement of Barb - strong person despite all the anxiety & fear"
- "Being able to relate to some of the scenarios others described during introductions"
- "Mutual respect and support; enjoying the organized format with time for discussion"
- "Hoarding is such an embarrassing habit/'sin' that it's good to be with other 'normal' people with the same issue"

There were only two "worst thing" comments in the area of interpersonal relationships, and the second one speaks to the value of the relationships:

- "I do feel sorry for them, but it's still difficult to follow long-winded, off-topic from participants. Their homes and thoughts are disorganized. God bless them and help them."
- "Missing members"

Outcomes

During the first group session we have members complete a variety of evaluation tools. The results of the week one evaluations are provided to the group members during the second group session. In the final group session we have members complete the same evaluation tools for comparison purposes. Here are one group member's results from April Lane Benson's *Who Needs Help? Three Ways to Know: Are You an Overshopper?* All client names are fictitious.

Valence Compulsive Buying Scale - Sally

1= strongly disagree; 5= strongly agree

Q	Pre-test	Post-test
1	2	2
2	4	2
3	2	1
4	4	4
5	4	4
6	4	4
7	4	4
8	3	4
9	2	1
10	4	4
11	3	3
Total	**36**	**33**

If your score is 36 or higher you are likely to be a compulsive buyer.

Richmond Compulsive Buying Scale - Sally

<table>
<tr><th>Q</th><th>Pre-test</th><th>Post-test</th><th></th></tr>
<tr><td>1</td><td>3</td><td>1</td><td rowspan="4">1= strongly disagree; 7= strongly agree</td></tr>
<tr><td>2</td><td>2</td><td>1</td></tr>
<tr><td>3</td><td>2</td><td>1</td></tr>
<tr><td>4</td><td>4</td><td>2</td></tr>
<tr><td>5</td><td>4</td><td>2</td><td rowspan="2">1= never; 5= very often</td></tr>
<tr><td>6</td><td>4</td><td>4</td></tr>
<tr><td>Total</td><td>19</td><td>11</td><td></td></tr>
</table>

If your score is 25 or higher you almost need help.

Both of Sally's scales show decreases in self-identified compulsive buying behaviors. According to the scoring directions of the Valence scale, Sally started the Fresh Start program at the low threshold for being a compulsive buyer, and she completed the group below that same threshold. In the Richmond scale, Sally never met the identified score for needing help with her buying behaviors, and she was able to reduce her score further by the last group session.

The Savings Cognitions Inventory (Steketee, G., Frost, R.O., & Kyrios, M. (2003) asks those completing the evaluation to rate how often they had particular thoughts in the past week when trying to discard items. The tool is scored using four subscales: emotional attachment, memory, control, and responsibility. Below are two examples of results from the Savings Cognitions Inventory. Each graph shows the results from the first group and the last group displayed in columns. The upper horizontal line that runs across each column shows the typical subscale scores for hoarding clients, and the lower horizontal line shows the typical subscale scores for the community control subjects.

Carol's outcomes provide excellent examples of how we use data to improve the Fresh Start experience and to benefit members. On Carol's graph you can see that her control and responsibility scores declined, while her emotional attachment and memory scores increased. Carol's control score was brought below the line typical for hoarding, however her emotional attachment score started markedly above the hoarding line and ended even higher. While the group was unable to positively impact this subscale, it should be noted that Carol missed three sessions. Beginning with the subsequent groups, we began requiring members who miss sessions to make them up with one of us prior to the following group.

The second way in which outcomes are used is to inform treatment planning. Carol was well aware of her strong emotional attachment to the items of her two young children and the role played by her strong desire for another child despite. Carol's

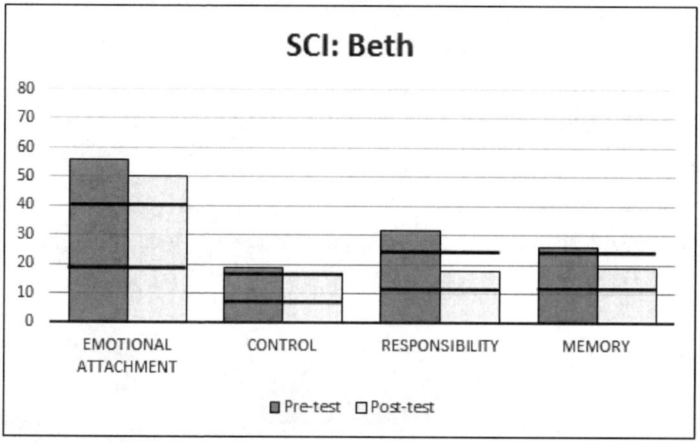
SCI: Beth
80
70
60
50
40
30
20
10
0
EMOTIONAL ATTACHMENT
CONTROL
RESPONSIBILITY
MEMORY
Pre-test
Post-test

therapy began to focus on these losses and that led to work on childhood trauma. The work with the professional organizer became focused on ways to manage those areas that housed the greatest emotional attachment.

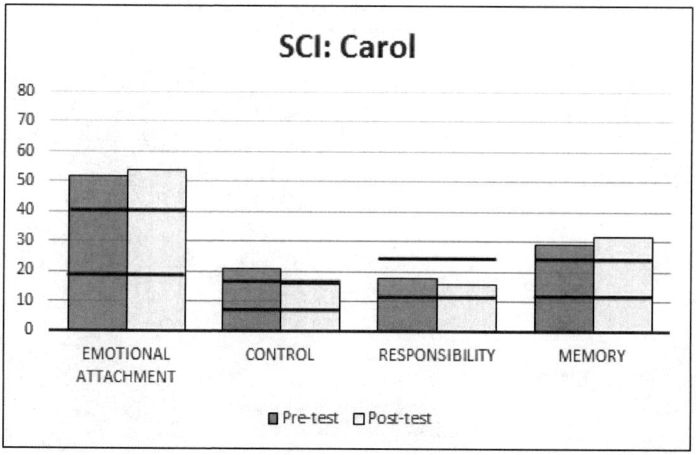
SCI: Carol
80
70
60
50
40
30
20
10
0
EMOTIONAL ATTACHMENT
CONTROL
RESPONSIBILITY
MEMORY
Pre-test
Post-test

The outcomes displayed in Beth's graph below show improvement in each of the four subscales. Beth attended every session and presented as a model group member, equally giving and receiving difficult feedback. While all her subscale scores except memory began and stayed above the hoarding line, the change in Beth was easily recognized in her organizing sessions with Karen. She worked with Karen before starting the Fresh Start group and then took roughly six months off prior to the group and six months off after she completed the group. When Beth resumed her organizing sessions, she displayed a dramatically reduced perfectionism, particularly in the areas of recycling and donating. She also embraced "good enough" as her new mantra.

Using session evaluations and outcome measures are important ways to ensure that the group model is effective and to suggest areas for improvement. It also helps the therapist monitor the subjective experiences of group members and aid treatment planning outside of the group.

11

FRESH START AND BEYOND

Fresh Start and Beyond developed as a response to group members' repeated requests to have an option to continue to work in a group setting on their issues related to hoarding and chronic disorganization. We provided the opportunity for all those who completed the eight week Fresh Start group to meet with us to brainstorm the options for a follow-up group. Based on their feedback, we began offering an optional monthly group to all graduates of Fresh Start. We named these graduate groups Fresh Start and Beyond.

The schedule for the year is given to members when they complete the eight week program, and a reminder/RSVP request email (blind-copied) is sent a few weeks prior to the scheduled session. We ask interested members to RSVP in order to ensure that the group room can accomodate the number of people interested. Anyone who prefers to be taken off the group email list is removed when they reply indicating that desire.

To further accommodate the needs of Fresh Start graduates, every quarter we rotate the day of the week on which the group meets, as indicated in this excerpt from the Fresh Start and Beyond schedule:

- 1st Quarter groups are on the first Saturdays of the month from 9:30 to 11:00, with the first half hour being optional social time
- 2nd Quarter groups are on the first Tuesdays of the month from 6:00 to 7:30, with the first half hour being optional social time
- 3rd Quarter groups are on the first Mondays of the month (September group meets on the second Monday) from 6:00 to 7:30, with the first half hour being optional social time
- 4th Quarter groups are on the first Saturdays of the month from 9:30 to 11:00, with the first half hour being optional social time

Each session is an hour long psychotherapy group with a different topic each month. We allow members to access the group room thirty minutes before the official start time so that interested attendees can have social time. The current topics are:

January – Kick off the new year by celebrating National Be On-Purpose Month and National Get Organized Month. We will look at the goals we have set for our year and develop plans to help keep us accountable.

February – No one complains they have too much time and not enough to do. National Time Management Month reminds us that difficulty managing how we spend our time can aggravate clutter and disorganization. Since it is also Relationship Wellness Month, we will discuss how time management affects our most important relationships.

March – People who struggle with clutter have creative gifts, including the ability to generate endless possibilities for using something. National Craft Month could be the harbinger of clutter. This month we will talk about how all that creativity gets in the way and develop strategies that help.

April – Addictions present lifelong challenges, whether the addiction is to alcohol, drugs, shopping, gambling, overeating, etc. This month is Emotional Overeating Awareness Month and Alcohol Awareness Month, but we will examine any addiction faced by group members and discuss 12-step groups for clutterers.

May – Fibromyalgia Education and Awareness Month and Women's Health Care Month help bring attention to the myriad of physical conditions affecting women. We will talk about how physical challenges make staying organized more challenging and learn skills to cope and celebrate National Meditation Month.

June – is PTSD Awareness Month. Deepen your understanding of the symptoms, learn how trauma may be affecting you, and gain tools for coping.

July – Families are great…most of the time! Family Reunion Month and Sandwich Generation Month set the stage for us to talk about setting limits with family members.

August – Join us as we uncover our vision for our lives. It is What Will Be Your Legacy Month and Happiness Happens Month, so we will be looking far down the road at what we want as well as how happiness happens every day.

September – is Attention Deficit Hyperactivity Disorder Month. Whether you have ADD, ADHD, or live with someone who does, this month will give you practical tips and tools to make life easier.

October – Even though it is Right Brainers Rule! Month, we think left brainers are great too. Join us as we dive deeper into the effects our thoughts have on our emotions, and learn how to get along better with people who think differently than we do. You'll celebrate Positive Attitude Month and increase your understanding of EQ during Emotional Intelligence Awareness Month.

November – Grief and loss are inevitable. This month National Family Caregivers Month and Family Stories Month inspire us to talk about loss through death or other circumstances, and its impact on our relationship with stuff.

December – December is Universal Human Rights Month, so exercise your right to get rid of something in your house through a "white elephant" gift exchange. Discussion will focus on how we protect and exercise our rights in relationships.

We typically have five to eight people attending each month. New graduates of the eight week program attending their first Fresh Start and Beyond group are greeted warmly by returning members. Initially we were worried about how the groups would function with a different mix of members each month. The first few Fresh Start and Beyond sessions convinced us that there was littleabout which to worry. Attendees quickly bonded based on their struggles with chronic disorganization and hoarding, along with their shared experiences attending the eight week program.

Currently, we are considering adding follow-up evaluation tools for those members who attend Fresh Start and Beyond groups.

PART 2

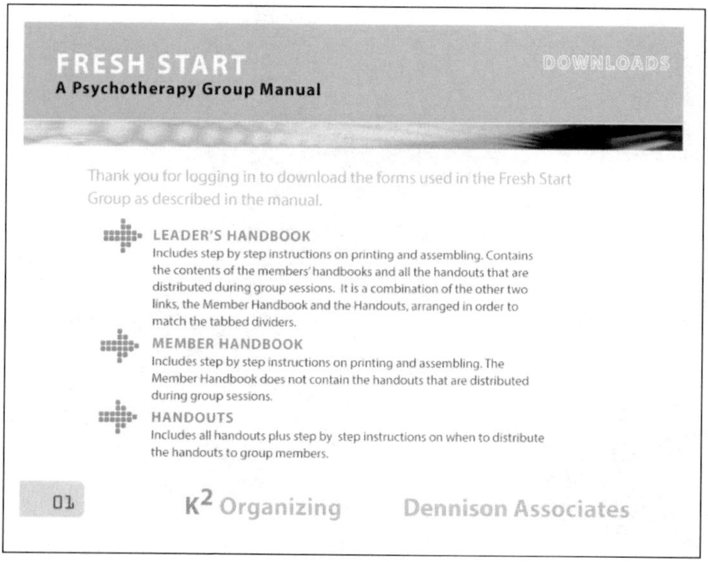
FRESH START
A Psychotherapy Group Manual
DOWNLOADS
Thank you for logging in to download the forms used in the Fresh Start Group as described in the manual.
LEADER'S HANDBOOK
Includes step by step instructions on printing and assembling. Contains the contents of the members' handbooks and all the handouts that are distributed during group sessions. It is a combination of the other two links, the Member Handbook and the Handouts, arranged in order to match the tabbed dividers.
MEMBER HANDBOOK
Includes step by step instructions on printing and assembling. The Member Handbook does not contain the handouts that are distributed during group sessions.
HANDOUTS
Includes all handouts plus step by step instructions on when to distribute the handouts to group members.
01
K2 Organizing
Dennison Associates

2.1 Downloadable Forms

On the following pages you will find the contents of the leader's handbook. You can download these pages and the instructions for assembling the leader's and group members' binders from:

www.k2organizing.com/FreshStartItems.

The only difference between the leader's and the group members' binders is that the leader's version includes handouts that are given out during particular group sessions. Those handouts are identified in the website download instructions.

GROUP LEADER'S HANDBOOK

2.2 Goals & Progress Log

Week 1: Date ____________

One small goal I will complete before next week is:

Week 2: Date ____________

Outcome of my goal and things that went well since the last week:

One small goal I will complete before next week is:

Week 3: Date ____________

Outcome of my goal and things that went well since the last week:

One small goal I will complete before next week is:

Week 4: Date ____________

Outcome of my goal and things that went well since the last week:

One small goal I will complete before next week is:

Week 5: Date ____________

Outcome of my goal and things that went well since the last week:

One small goal I will complete before next week is:

Week 6: Date ____________

Outcome of my goal and things that went well since the last week:

One small goal I will complete before next week is:

Week 7: Date ____________

Outcome of my goal and things that went well since the last week:

One small goal I will complete before next week is:

Week 8: Date ____________

Outcome of my goal and things that went well since the last week:

2.3 Evaluating the Problem

A. Assessments

- ☐ Savings Cognitions Inventory
- ☐ Savings Inventory – Modified Format
- ☐ Hoarding Rating Scale
- ☐ Institute for Challenging Disorganization's (ICD) "Are You Situationally Disorganized?"
- ☐ Institute for Challenging Disorganization's (ICD) "Are You Chronically Disorganized?"
- ☐ Institute for Challenging Disorganization's (ICD) Clutter – Hoarding Rating Scale
- ☐ April Lane Benson, Ph.D. Stopping Overshopping, LLC's "Who Needs Help? Three Ways to Know: Are You an Overshopper?"
- ☐ Post-Traumatic Stress Disorder Checklist
- ☐ Acute Stress Disorder Scale
- ☐ Trauma History Scale

B. Common Characteristics of Chronic Disorganization and/or Hoarding

Accumulation of possessions
Variety of hobbies/interests
Distractability
Distress and/or impairment
Reliance on visual reminders
Time awareness
Difficulty discrading

With which characteristics of chronic disorganization or haording do you struggle the most? Describe how they affect you.

C. Evaluation of group session

What was the best thing about today's group?

What was the worst thing about today's group?

D. Homework

Clutter-Image Rating Scale - Fill in your ratings (1-9) below for each room from www.ocfoundation.org/hoarding/cir.pdf

Location	Ratings
Kitchen	
Living Room	
Bedroom 1	
Bedroom 2	
Basement	
Garage	
Dining Room	
Other ___________	
Other ___________	

2.4 The Brain's Role: Thinking Patterns

A. Positive reports and review of homework

B. Cognitive distortions

All or nothing thinking
Overgeneralization
Mental filter
Personalization and blame
Jumping to conclusions
Magnification/Minimalizations
Emotional reasoning
"Should" statements
Labeling
Discounting positives

List your most common cognitive distortions

C. Negative self-talk

Worrier
Critic
Victim
Perfectionist

List your most common self-talk

D. Effective cognitive coping tools and tips

- Catch your thinking errors as they occur
- Look for exceptions to black and white thinking
- Consider other ways of thinking about situations
- Ask yourself whether you would hold yourself to the same standards as you do yourself
- Use postive self talk: remind yourself that there can be an end to this
- Recognize worry as your cue to consider taking action. If there is nothing you can do about a situation, practice acceptance
- Be aware of a tendency to be critical of yourself

- Do you judge others are harshly as you judge yourself? If not, why not?
- Picture an elderly you; what would she think of you?
- When you catch yourself, replace the negative self-talk with positive self-talk that focuses on your accomplishments and abilities and does not expect a standard you would not expect from someone else

E. Evaluation of group session

What was the best thing about today's group?

What was the worst thing about today's group?

F. Homework

Clutter-Image Rating Scale - Fill in your ratings (1-9) below for each room from www.ocfoundation.org/hoarding/cir.pdf

Location	Ratings
Kitchen	
Living Room	
Bedroom 1	
Bedroom 2	
Basement	
Garage	
Dining Room	
Other ____________	
Other ____________	

Review of directions for the cognitive distortion card: On the front of an index card under the heading "Automatic Thought", write an example of one automatic you had. Below that, under "Cognitive Distortion" identify which cognitive distortions your thought represents. On the back of the card is the heading "Rational Response". After challenging your thinking and developing at least one rational response, write these on the back of the index card.

Which cognitive distortion did you put on your card? How was it to come up with a rational response?

Which negative self-talk did you catch yourself thinking? What did you do to correct it?

Which cognitive coping tools were most effective for you? Try one new one and put the results here.

2.5 Cognitive Distortions Overview

Please review the ten common cognitive distortions to get a general understanding. People who tend to be highly literal or perfectionistic often struggle with their need to fit examples neatly into one cognitive distortion or another. It can be difficult to handle the ambiguity of thoughts that might be examples of more than one cognitive distortion. Those who are chronically disorganized or hoard can be helped to recognize that the most important part is recognizing the thinking error and then correcting it, rather than what name the distortion should be given. Examples are provided of how these are typically displayed by chronically disorganized and hoarding clients.

1. All-or-nothing thinking – People often establish a goal that only serves to set them up for failure. They will often say "I need to organize my whole house this weekend" or "I will always follow the only-handle-it-once (OHIO) rule." What can happen when people set out to follow the OHIO rule without exception is that they run into an item about which they are not ready to decide. Instead of making an exception to the rule and creating a "to be decided' pile, they completely abandon their organizing efforts.

2. Overgeneralization: Statements like "I can never find anything" only serve to stop those with chronic disorganization and hoarding from discovering what works for them and then building off those strategies. People who focus on the regrets they have about items they have thrown out or donated can see the fit with this cognitive distortion.

3. Discounting positives: "Why bother? When I am working on one area of my house, another gets

worse." We all feel this way at times. A more helpful thought includes recognition that there are periods of disorganization, and that maintenance is just another part of the process.

4. Jumping to conclusions: This distortion involves either mind reading or fortune telling. Commonly heard is a combination of both "I can spend hours organizing the kitchen and my husband will come home and say 'what about the bedroom?'"

5. Should statements: These have a way of generating the exact opposite of what the chronically disorganized and hoarding client expects. If they are imposing a rule (I should), then it should happen. What they do not realize, is that these are judgments disguised as rules. Should statements either make a person feel superior if they complete the "should" or feel like a failure if they don't. People with chronic disorganization or hoarding often say things like "I should be more organized" or "I should be able to do this myself".

6. Personalization and blame: A person might take the criticism from a partner that their child does not keep their room clean because they are a bad example. We hear people blaming themselves for the death of a pet who had a diagnosable illness. They might say I stopped going through that part of the house since ..... died. Others do not accept self-responsibility and overlook ways that they are contributing to the problem.

7. Labeling: People assign meaning or accept the name-calling of others; "I am a slob", instead of saying I have developed sloppy behaviors that I would like to change.

8. Emotional reasoning: When we determine truth by feeling states we have no objective view. Examples include: "I feel like a crazy person, so I know I am crazy."

9. Magnifying or minimizing: People sometimes exaggerate or underrate how disorganized a room really is. "It is a disaster!" or "it is not that bad, I can still live there." It is not unusual when living among clutter to become anesthetized to the negative psychological and physical ramifications.

10. Mental Filter: When a person reports and thinks about the negatives, they can overlook the positives. Every day ask yourself what went well yesterday? This technique helps to turn off the mental filter.

Adopted from David Burns MD,
10 Cognitive Distortions

2.6 Cognitive Distortions Index Card Samples

Card Front

Automatic Thought

I can't get rid of these bags. I should find a use for them.

Cognitive Distortions

Should Statements
Jumping to Conclusions

Card Back

Rational Response

Although it is likely to be difficult to get rid of these bags,
I can do it.

2.7 The Brain's Role: Executive Functions

A. Positive reports and review of homework

B. Weak or overloaded executive functions

Attention	Planning & Initiation
Decision-making	Organization & Categorization
Memory	Metacognition

With which executive functions do you struggle most?

C. Strategies to improve executive functioning

- Use a master to do list instead of visual cues
- Experiment with decision making and see if the outcome is as bad as you imagine
- Think of a time when you were able to sustain attention on a difficult or unpleasant task. What was different? Can you replicate any of those conditions that led to success?
- Would it be helpful to have another person work with you on a plan or get you started?
- Start with a few broad categories and don't be afraid of an "undecided" category
- Instead of asking what you can do with something, ask if you will. If you will, give yourself a deadline

D. Evaluation of group session

What was the best thing about today's group?

What was the worst thing about today's group?

E. Homework

Clutter-Image Rating Scale - Fill in your ratings (1-9) below for each room from www.ocfoundation.org/hoarding/cir.pdf

Location	Ratings
Kitchen	
Living Room	
Bedroom 1	
Bedroom 2	
Basement	
Garage	
Dining Room	
Other ____________	
Other ____________	

How do you think your life would be different if you had improvement in one or more executive functions?

Which strategies to improve executive functioning were most effective for you? Try one new one and put the results here.

2.8 The Brain's Role: Other Cognitive Factors

A. Postive reports and review of homework

B. Other cognitive factors

- Elaborative Processing
- Beliefs about Use, Waste, and Responsibility
- Beliefs about Identity
- Procrastination
    - Moods
    - Cognitions
    - Practicalities

List the most frequent causes of your procrastination.

C. Effective strategies for cognitive factors

- Focus more on the larger goal of de-cluttering or organizing a space and less on the smaller goals of recycling and donating
- Ask yourself whether you need objects to make you who you are
- When you find yourself procrastinating, figure out the cause and develop a workable strategy
- Set a timer for 10 or 20 minutes and work on organizing for only that amount of time
- Tackle the most difficult thing first – bite the head off the frog – so the rest of the day or time period is based on an early success and the big thing no longer weighs on you.
- Use fun activities as rewards for completing things that are not interesting but still important
- Eliminate as many distractions as possible – both internal (hunger, thirst, fatigue) and external (kids, phone, TV)

- Batch your activities. Check your email a few times each day rather than throughout the day; make your calls all in the same block of time; file papers in a batch, not as they come in.
- Downward Arrow

D. Evaluation of group session

What was the best thing about today's group?

What was the worst thing about today's group?

E. Homework

Clutter-Image Rating Scale - Fill in your ratings (1-9) below for each room from www.ocfoundation.org/hoarding/cir.pdf

Location	Ratings
Kitchen	
Living Room	
Bedroom 1	
Bedroom 2	
Basement	
Garage	
Dining Room	
Other ___________	
Other ___________	

How do you see the "Other Cognitive Factors" (elaborative processing; beliefs about usefulness, waste, and responsibility; beliefs about identity; procrastination) of the handout affecting you?

Which strategies for improving other cognitive factors from Section C of the handout were most effective for you? Try one new one and put the results here.

2.9 Procrastination

Causes of Procrastination

1. **Feelings/Moods**
   - The task is unpleasant
   - You feel overwhelmed
   - You are not in the mood
   - You don't want the responsibility
   - You fear success
   - You "thrive" on the adrenalin rush caused by waiting until the last minute
2. **Thoughts/Cognitions**
   - The task is too difficult
   - The goals are unclear
   - It seems unimportant
   - It might go away
   - You need time to mull it over
3. **Behaviors/Practicalities**
   - Interruptions
   - Disorganization
   - A lack of information
   - Not enough time
   - It isn't due for a while
   - You want to do it perfectly

Strategies to Overcome Procrastination

1. **If the task is unpleasant**
   - Play music
   - Use a pleasing scent to fill your work area
   - Make up some games that involve steps of the task
   - Plan something fun for when you are done

2. **If you feel overwhelmed**
   - Break the task down into smaller parts
   - Recall times when you have completed other tasks even when they seemed overwhelming initially
   - Stay focused on the vision of what to achieve

3. **If you are not in the mood**
    - Ask yourself if you need to be in the mood to start the task
    - Work for 10 minutes and see if you can get past the mood and if not, stop for a while

4. **If you don't want the responsibility**
    - Determine if you fear failure, delegate when possible

5. **If you fear success**
    - Figure out what you fear about success
    - Do small things that move you closer to success and see how you feel

6. **If you "thrive" on the adrenalin rush caused by waiting until the last minute**
    - Try exercising and then begin the task
    - Plan a (safe) alternative adrenaline rush as a reward if you finish the task early

7. **If the task is too difficult**
    - Ask yourself if it really is too difficult or that is your fear or low self-esteem talking
    - If it really is too difficult, determine which parts are too difficult and what you need to make them easier
    - If you need more information, get it
    - If you need expert assistance, either delegate it or hire an expert
    - If the task is more than a one person job, get help

8. **If the goals are unclear**
    - Either begin the task and hope the goals become clearer, or determine how to get clarity
    - If the task is assigned to you, go back to the assignor and ask for clarification
    - If the task is of your own making, ask yourself why it needs to be done
    - You can challenge the reasons if they include words like "should", 'ought", or "must"
    - Why should you? What are the consequences if you don't?

9. **If the task seems unimportant**
    - Determine the consequences of not doing it
    - Does it make sense to be completed this task, or are there other more important tasks that need to be done instead?

10. **If it might go away**
    - Is that really true?
    - Are there negative consequences if it "goes away"?
    - If it is not true or there are unwanted consequences, does procrastinating make the tasks easier in any way?

11. **If you need time to mull it over**
    - There may be nothing wrong with that, and it may not even mean you are procrastinating
    - You can schedule a time to be alone and mull over the task
    - It may be helpful to give yourself a deadline to end the deliberating time and start the acting time.

12. **Interruptions**
    - Allow more time than you think you need to complete the task
    - Minimize interruptions by turning off visual and audio alerts on electronic devises
    - Make sure you have eaten and are hydrated
    - Purge your working memory by writing down everything you can think of – things you have to do, ideas you want to remember, and random thoughts
    - Keep paper handy so you can write down anything that pops into your head while you are working on your task

13. **Disorganization**
    - Clear the area where you will be working
    - Don't worry about getting everything put away unless it will take less than 5 minutes
    - Make a list of all the supplies you need for your task and then gather them into the location where you will be working.

14. Lack of Information

- Make a list of all the information you need and then one by one figure out how to get the information
- Do you need to look in a filing cabinet? Search the internet? Ask someone else? If you are not sure how to get the information, how can you find out how to get the information?

15. Not Enough Time

- Break the task down into small parts
- There might be researching, shopping for supplies, or doing a small part of a larger job, such as cleaning out a drawer for the larger job of cleaning out a desk
- If there still is not enough time, put each part on your calendar for a later date

16. It Isn't Due for a While

- Break the task into parts and schedule each
- Schedule some type of reward for yourself after completing each part on time
- Also, you can schedule the parts of the task immediately before a scheduled event you enjoy so that you can't start the enjoyable activity until the part of the task is completed.

17. You Want to Do it Perfectly

- Recognize that you will never achieve perfection and determine what is "good enough"
- If you procrastinate long enough you will rush to get it done and you will do a sub-par job
- Telling yourself that it was only because you did it at the last minute or in a hurry is really a cop out
- Free yourself by getting it done imperfectly instead of having it hanging out there waiting to be done

2.10 Downward Arrow Worksheet

This technique is useful to help you discover what core beliefs and fear systems influence your saving or acquiring behaviors. To challenge your core belief related to discarding an item or diminishing acquiring:

1. My cognition (thought) about what is bothering me or my family about my situation:

2. What does this mean about me?

3. How honestly believable is this representation of me is on a scale of 1 to 10, with one being I am not like that at all and ten being absolutely true.

Repeat the process until you arrive at the core belief. It is often what you have been taught about something that actually causes your discomfort. Ex: Waste not want not. Try to repeat the process until you find your core belief rating on the 1 to 10 scale closer to 1.

Next challenge your feelings about sorting, discarding an item, or reducing your acquiring.

4. The unpleasant feelings that I think I would feel if I parted with an item:

5. The worst thing that could happen if I feel this way?

6. Rate this feeling from 1 to 10 with one being barely noticeable to 10 being extreme panic or debilitating depression:

7. Repeat this process until the feeling is near or at a 1 on the scale.

2.11 Emotional and Physical Factors

A. Postive reports and reveiew of homework

B. Acquiring

- Passive
- Active
- Questions to ask yourself

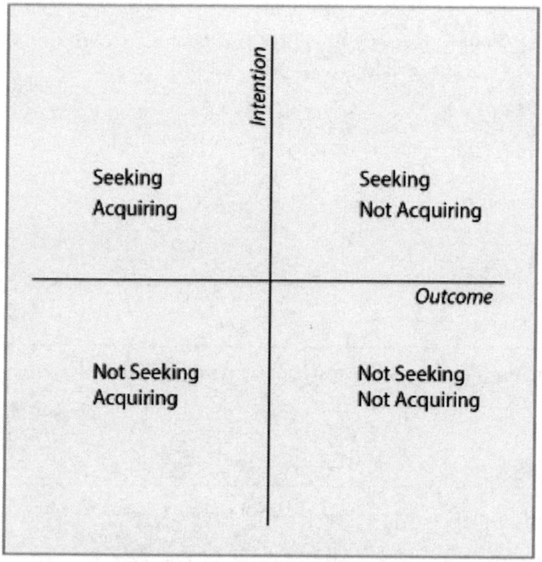
Intention
Seeking
Acquiring
Seeking
Not Acquiring
Outcome
Not Seeking
Acquiring
Not Seeking
Not Acquiring

Do you struggle more with active or passive acquiring?

Non-Acquiring Tips

- When you are shopping determine your emotional state prior to purchases to ensure you are shopping for need and not to manage emotions
- Write down your feelings prior to a purchase and determine if the purchase is still a good choice for you

- When you are shopping, it is okay to put things in your cart. Before you check out, re- evaluate each item to determine if you really need it
- It is okay to enjoy the hunt for something, find it, and then not buy it
- Before you purchase, have a plan for using the item soon and a place to store it
- Remember that just because you found something free, on sale, or useful does not mean that it is good for you to get it
- Stay focused on your goals and vision for your life
- Good deals tend to repeat themselves
- Only pay with cash; leave your wallet in the car

C. Common Emotional Factors

Depression
Fear
Trauma
Hopelessness
Anxiety
Emotional attachment to "stuff"

Which emotional factors most influence your ability to be organized?

D. Common Physical Factors

Chronic pain
Arthritis
Fatigue
Fibromyalgia
Visual impairment
HALT
Obesity
Chronic Illness

Which physical factors most infulence your ability to be organized?

E. Healthy Self-Soothing Tools

Guided imagery
Mindfulness
Support person
Deep breath work
Viewing containment
Hot bath
Petting an animal
Scent of a favorite candle
Hypnotherapy
Journaling
Exercising
Music

Which self-soothing tools do you already use?

F. Evaluation of group session

What was the best thing about today's group?

What was the worst thing about today's group?

G. Homework

Clutter-Image Rating Scale - Fill in your ratings (1-9) below for each room from www.ocfoundation.org/hoarding/cir.pdf

Location	Ratings
Kitchen	
Living Room	
Bedroom 1	
Bedroom 2	
Basement	
Garage	
Dining Room	
Other ____________	
Other ____________	

During the week did you have times when you were able to decline from either active or passive acquiring? Describe the situation here.

What was the outcome of the new self-soothing tools you tried?

2.12 The Influence of Personality Type: DISC Model

A. Positive Reports and Review of Homework

B. DISC Model

- **D**irecting - Just do it
- **I**nfluencing - Have fun doing it
- **S**upportive - Do it together
- **C**ontemplative - Do it right

Which DISC trait do you most recognize in yourself?

Knowing more about your personality style, what do you need to help you de-clutter, reduce acquiring, and/or get organized?

C. Evaluation of group session

What was the best thing about today's group?

What was the worst thing about today's group?

D. Homework

Clutter-Image Rating Scale - Fill in your ratings (1-9) below for each room from www.ocfoundation.org/hoarding/cir.pdf

Location	Ratings
Kitchen	
Living Room	
Bedroom 1	
Bedroom 2	
Basement	
Garage	
Dining Room	
Other ____________	
Other ____________	

What additional questions or insight do you have about the DISC personality types?

2.13 DISC Assesment

1. In the space below, determine those behaviors in each row that are MOST to LEAST like your behaviors. Work from left to right.

4	3	2	1
MOST like you	next most like you	next least like you	LEAST like you

2. Use each number **only once in each row**

Column 1	Column 2	Column 3	Column 4
Direct	Influencing	Steady	Cautious
Self-assured	Optimistic	Deliberate	Restrained
Adventurous	Enthusiastic	Perdictable	Logical
Decisive	Open	Patient	Analytical
Daring	Impulsive	Team player	Accurate
Forceful	Sensitive	Sincere	Perfectionist
Risk-taking	Poised	Easy-going	Consistent
Assertive	Talkative	Modest	Diplomatic
Competitive	Persuasive	Accommodating	Curious
Restless	Emotional	Protective	Doubting
Total ____	**Total** ____	**Total** ____	**Total** ____

3. Add your scores in each column. Place the totals in the blanks at the bottom of each column. When all four totals are added together, they should equal 100.

4. If your highest total is in:

- Column 1, your primary style is Driving-Directing
- Column 2, your primary style is Influencing-Expressive
- Column 3, your primary style is Steady-Amiable/Supportive
- Column 4, your primary style is Cautious-Analytical/Contemplating

This assessment is designed to understand your style as it relates toward tendencies and not absolutes. It should be regarded only as one indicator in the total makeup and environment of an individual. It is designed to help you better understand your behaviors and those of others.

2.14 DISC Quadrant Model

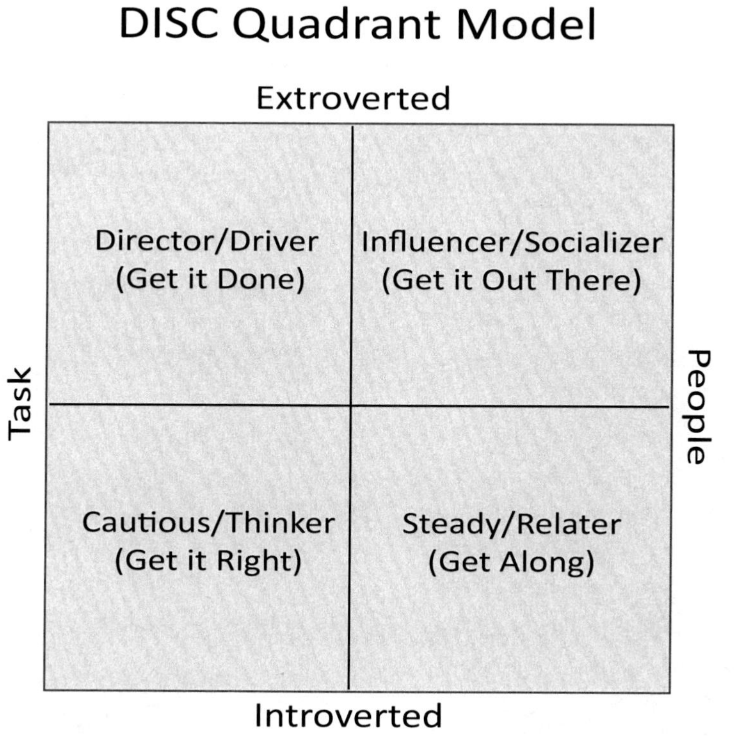
DISC Quadrant Model
Extroverted
Director/Driver
(Get it Done)
Influencer/Socializer
(Get it Out There)
Task
People
Cautious/Thinker
(Get it Right)
Steady/Relater
(Get Along)
Introverted

2.15 DISC Traits

D Traits

- Very active in dealing with problems and challenges
- Demanding
- Forceful, Aggressive
- Egocentric
- Strong-willed
- Driving, determined
- Determined
- Ambitious, pioneering
- Fast-paced
- Impatient
- Controlling
- Big-picture oriented
- Competitive
- Quick to judge
- Takes risks
- Likes to tell rather than be told
- Motivators – Power and authority, immediate results, new challenges

I Traits

- Influence others through talking and activity, demonstrative
- Emotional
- Convincing, persuasive
- Magnetic
- Enthusiastic
- Warm
- Trusting
- Impulsive
- Optimistic
- Outgoing
- Dynamic language
- Envisions, Dreams
- Needs to work with others
- Fast-paced
- Motivators – Social recognition, freedom of expression, high energy associates

S Traits

- Want security, do not like sudden change
- Calm, patient
- Relaxed
- Possessive
- Predictable
- Deliberate
- Stable, consistent
- Warm, open
- Emotional
- Good listener
- Slow to confront
- Responds to pressure by giving in
- Easily hurt
- Loyal
- Slow-paced
- Motivators – traditions, stability, cooperation

C Traits

- Adhere to rules, regulations, and structure
- Like to do quality work and do it right the first time
- Careful, cautious
- Exacting, accurate
- Neat, orderly
- Systematic
- Diplomatic, tactful
- Undemonstrative, impersonal
- Quiet
- Conservative
- Efficient
- Slow to decide
- Likes facts and information
- Rational problem-solving approach
- Slow-paced
- Motivators – data, accurate information, systems/procedures/rules, reassurance

2.16 DISC Communication Strategies

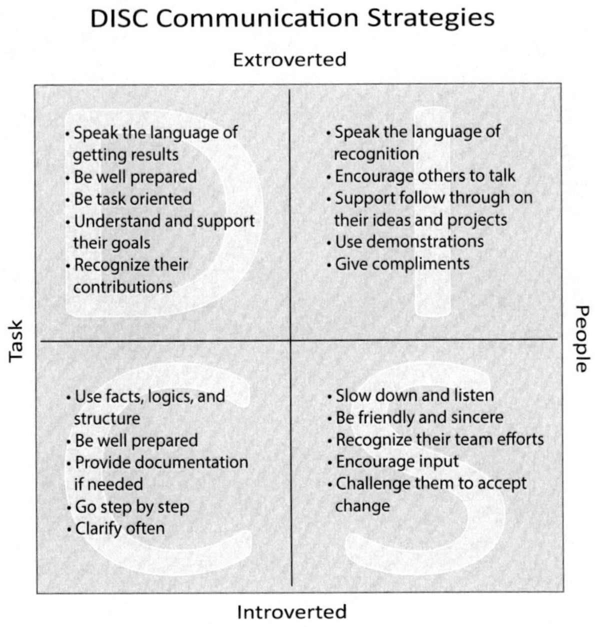
DISC Communication Strategies
Extroverted
Introverted
Task
People
• Speak the language of getting results
• Be well prepared
• Be task oriented
• Understand and support their goals
• Recognize their contributions
• Speak the language of recognition
• Encourage others to talk
• Support follow through on their ideas and projects
• Use demonstrations
• Give compliments
• Use facts, logics, and structure
• Be well prepared
• Provide documentation if needed
• Go step by step
• Clarify often
• Slow down and listen
• Be friendly and sincere
• Recognize their team efforts
• Encourage input
• Challenge them to accept change

2.17 The Influence of Personality Type: Myers-Briggs Type Indicator

A. Positive Reports and Review of Homework

B. Myers-Briggs Type Indicator

- **E**xtroverted or **I**ntroverted
- **S**ensing or i**N**tuitive
- **T**hinking or **F**eeling
- **J**udging or **P**erceiving

What Myers-Briggs personality type do you most recognize in yourself?

Knowing more about your personality style, what do you need to help you de-clutter, reduce acquiring, and/or get organized?

C. Evaluation of group session

What was the best thing about today's group?

What was the worst thing about today's group?

D. Homework

Clutter-Image Rating Scale - Fill in your ratings (1-9) below for each room from www.ocfoundation.org/hoarding/cir.pdf

Location	Ratings
Kitchen	
Living Room	
Bedroom 1	
Bedroom 2	
Basement	
Garage	
Dining Room	
Other ____________	
Other ____________	

What additional questions or insight do you have about the Myers-Briggs personality types?

2.18 Moving Forward

A. Positive Reports and Review of Homework

B. Wellness planning

C. Group Feedback

- Share with one or more group members something you learned from them specifically
- Share with one or more group members something you believe is a growth area for them specifically

D. Self-Hypnosis

- Benefits
  - Increases control of some functions, such as heart rate
  - Helps coping with pain
  - Produces anesthesia in any part of the body
  - Increases the capacity to remember and learn
  - Can master it within 2 days with practice
- How it works
  - Conscious mind is about 10% of our total mind. It thinks, analyzes, and has short-term memory. Habits are not stored in the conscious part of the mind.
  - Subconscious mind is involuntary and controls long term memory, creativity, emotions, sensory experiences, and habits. Habits are usually developed by giving the subconscious mind suggestions of what you would like to see change, i.e. hypnosis.
  - Visualize what you would like to see change, use breath work, picture throwing a stone into a well, and repeat "Calm and Relaxed".
  - Hypnosis can more than double the success rates of cognitive-behavioral treatment, and the impact of hypnosis increases over time.

2.19 Activity Homework: Part 1

Date: ______________

Choose an item to bring to the next group session

How would you feel if you let the chosen item go?

How long do you think it would take you to get over that feeling? __________________________

Rate the feeling 0-10, with 10 being the worst: ____

What bad outcome do you expect if you let the item go?

How long do you think it would take you to revover from that bad outcome? ________________________

Are you willing to leave the item with the group for a week?

During the week, please note the attachments that exist to that item.

2.20 Activity Homework: Part 2

Date: ______________

How did you feel letting the chosen item go?

Rate the feeling 0-10, with 10 being the worst: ____

How long did it take you to get over that feeling?

If you were worried that something bad would happen, did it? Did anything good happen?

If applicable, how long did it take you to recover from that bad outcome? ________________________________

During the week, please note the thoughts and feelings you had about the item.

What do you want to happen to the item now?

2.21 Wellness Plan

A. Lingering questions

In terms of active and passive acquiring from Emotional and Physical Factors session, I still need help understanding or more information about…

In terms of emotional factors that contribute to disorganization from Emotional and Physical Factors session, I still need help understanding or more information about…

In terms of physical factors that contribute to disorganization from Emotional and Physical Factors session, I still need help understanding or more information about…

In terms of self-soothing tools from Emotional and Physical Factors session, I still need help understanding or more information about…

In terms of the DISC model from The Influence of Personality Type: DISC Model session, I still need help understanding or more information about…

In terms of the Myers-Briggs model from The Influence of Personality Type: Myers-Briggs Type Indicator session, I still need help understanding or more information about…

In terms of cognitive distortions from The Brain's Role: Thinking Patterns session, I still need help understanding or more information about…

In terms of self-talk from The Brain's Role: Thinking Patterns session, I still need help understanding or more information about…

In terms of executive functions from weeks The Brain's Role: Executive Functions session, I still need help understanding or more information about…

In terms of the other cognitive factors from weeks The Brain's Role: Other Cognitive Factors session, I still need help understanding or more information about…

In terms of cognitive coping strategies from any of The Brain's Role sessions, I still need help understanding or more information about…

In terms of other things, I still need help understanding or more information about…

B. Stress

- Recognize your signs that stress is building. Notice your body's reactions and any desire to run away.
- Use the 3 P's of stress management:
    - Partialize (break things in parts; make lists or draw pictures of what you are stressed about)
    - Prioritize (rank things in order of importance; some things are important but not urgent)
    - Postpone (not everything has to be done right away; plan to put some things off)

My signs of stress are:

Things that trigger my stress are:

Things that I do to reduce stress in my life are:

Things that I will do to manage stress are:

C. De-cluttering

Things I need to be able to de-clutter (consider people, music, sleep, mood, etc.)

My de-cluttering goal:

I will know I am successful when:

Due date____

D. Organizing

Things I need to be able to get organized (consider supplies, ideas, time, help, etc.):

My organizing goal:

I will know I am successful when:

Due date____

E. Relapse

- Recognize that relapse is a normal part of any change
- To prevent relapse, take pictures of your home now and then again when each area is at its best
  - Look at the "before" pictures when you need motivation to keep going and realize that "relapse" does not have to mean going back to that state
  - Use the "after" pictures to remind yourself of the good feelings and success you experience in an organized space
- Reach out to family, friends, or professionals if you need help following the steps outlined in this plan before you get to the point of feeling overwhelmed
- Schedule an event at your house every month or so to help you stay on top of the clutter
- Recognize and acknowledge that progress is progress no matter the amount, so keep looking into a better future

My relapse prevention plan:

F. Other Tips and Tools

When and how to involve family or friends

- Decide what it is that you need from the person. Do you need them to sit quietly as you work? Do you need them to offer suggestions? Help you make decisions? Carry and move things? Follow your directions?
- Once you know what you need, think about the person you are considering. Does this seem like something they might be comfortable with and good at? Not everyone is good at helping you make decisions, but they might be good at carrying things for you.
- If you think you have a match for the task and the person, ask them if they are interested in helping you. If they are, explain the help you need and don't need. Make sure they know that if they are not up for what you are asking of them, they can opt out without negative consequences.

Getting focused and re-focused

- Make a date with yourself to work on de-cluttering or organizing. Plan on a specific amount of time to work – something manageable
- Focus on a small piece – one pile, one drawer, one shelf, etc.
- Face a wall while you work to eliminate visual distractions
- Experiment with playing different types of music or different scents to help you stay focused
- If you get distracted remind yourself of your goal for that time period and get back to it

Self-Care

You can't de-clutter or organize if you do not take care of yourself. Areas to look at are

- Exercise – start small and build. Get both strength-building and cardio exercises. Walk every day. Park far from your destination to easily add walking to your daily routine.
- Nutrition – Make fruits and vegetables the central part of every meal; limit caffeine, sugar, and simple carbohydrates
- Sleep – go to bed and get up at about the same time every day; keep your bedroom dark
- Memory – all three items listed above help our memories function at their best. Continue to work your brain and look for strategies to improve your memory
- Positive thoughts – about yourself and others; remember your gifts and accomplishments
- Saying No – Remind yourself that you do not need to say yes to everything. If someone offers you a good deal on something, think about how likely it is you will use that item. Also consider how you have managed without it and the "price" of storage and maintenance.
- Meditation, stretching, yoga – these will all boost your energy, re-focus you, and increase your ability to do more
- Socialization – reach out to or re-connect to one potential friend each month.
- Ask for help – recognize that no one is good at or has time for everything. As we age it becomes especially important to reach out for help in some areas

Donate/recycle resource list –This is a separate document provided to you in Box to assist you in your de-cluttering efforts.

APPENDIX & HANDOUTS

A. Preparing Letter

B. Acquiring/Discarding Cards

APPENDIX A: Preparing for Fresh Start Psychotherapy Group

Barbara Jo Dennison, PhD, LISW-S
Karen Kruzan LISW-S, CPO-CD

Welcome to the Fresh Start Group! We are excited to help you on your journey out of chronic disorganization or hoarding. To help you get the most out of the psychotherapy group, please read the information below, ask us any questions you have, and sign at the bottom to indicate your agreement to abide by these policies.

Confidentiality
Group members get the most benefit from psychotherapy when they are confident that what they say in group will not be shared with anyone outside of the group. By participating in the Fresh Start psychotherapy group you are agreeing to keep private the names and identifying information of fellow group members (names, jobs, family situations, etc.)

Attendance
You are expected to attend every group session. We understand that there are occasionally situations that cannot be avoided and you may miss a session. If that occurs, you will need to make up that group session in a sixty minute session with either Dr. Dennison or Ms. Kruzan.

Participation
Group members are expected to participate in the group conversations and share their thoughts and feelings. As group leaders, we may ask provocative questions or stop you from going off track or monopolizing the group. Feedback from fellow group members is an important part of any psychotherapy group. Group members are encouraged to provide both positive feedback and to challenge each other's thoughts and behaviors. As group leaders, we will do our best to create a safe

environment for members to address the issues that brought them to the group.

Materials

There are multiple handouts each week and you can choose to manage this in one of two ways:

1. You can bring a laptop or tablet that can connect to the internet, download the handouts during the group, and work off the electronic copies, OR

2. We will provide you with a binder, tabbed dividers, and all the handouts at a cost to you of $10.00.

Please indicate your choice here: _______

You will need to bring your binder or electronic device to each meeting. All materials will be available on www.box.com in a folder only accessible to members in your group session. If you want access to the on-line folder, an email invitation will be sent to you. Please write your email address here if you want this access and you understand that other group members will be able to see your email address: ______________________________

Homework

In order to maximize the benefit of the Fresh Start psychotherapy group, it is important for you to complete all homework assignments before the subsequent group session. If you have questions about the homework, you can contact either Dr. Dennison or Ms. Kruzan for clarification

APPENDIX B: Acquiring/Discarding Decision Cards

To order Acquiring/Discarding Decision Cards, contact:

Karen Kruzan
at kkruzan@k2organzing.com
or 614.795.0626.

The cards are available in coated or laminated versions. Both options provide durability, and the laminated version allows the client to use and reuse a dry erase marker on the Yes/No boxes.

Discounts are available for bulk purchases.

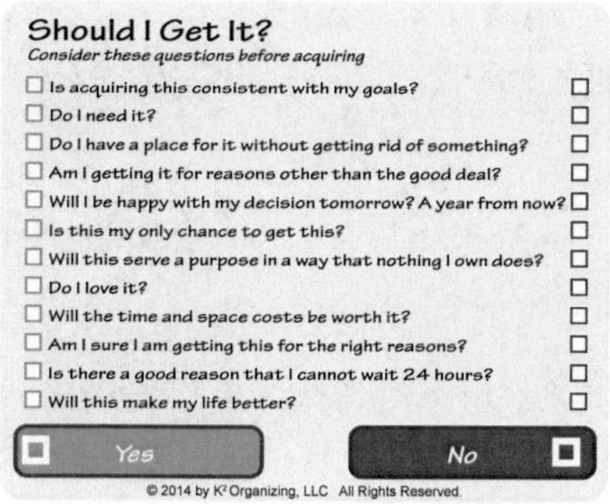
Should I Get It?
Consider these questions before acquiring
Is acquiring this consistent with my goals?
Do I need it?
Do I have a place for it without getting rid of something?
Am I getting it for reasons other than the good deal?
Will I be happy with my decision tomorrow? A year from now?
Is this my only chance to get this?
Will this serve a purpose in a way that nothing I own does?
Do I love it?
Will the time and space costs be worth it?
Am I sure I am getting this for the right reasons?
Is there a good reason that I cannot wait 24 hours?
Will this make my life better?
Yes
No
© 2014 by K² Organizing, LLC All Rights Reserved

Resources

Baranowsky, Anna, Gentry, Eric, Schultz, Frankin. (2011). Trauma Practice Tools for Stabilization/Recovery. Cambridge, MA: Hogrefe Publishing.

Burns, D. (1993). Ten Days to Self Esteem. New York, NY, William Morrow and Company, Inc.

Carlson, Eve. (2013, Sept.).Assessing Trauma Survivors Risk Profiles and Using Them to Foster Resilience.

Dennison, B., Kruzan, K., (2013). The Many Faces of Hoarding and Trauma, DVD., Columbus, Ohio, AVS Video Publications.

Diagnostic and Statistical Manual of Mental Disorders, Fifth Edition, (2013). American Psychiatric Association.

Foa, E.B., Keane, T.M., Friedman, M.S., & Cohen J.A. (2009). Effective Treatments for PTSD: Practice guidelines of the International Society For Traumatic Stress Studies. New York, NY: Guilford Press.

Frost, R.O. &Steketee, G. (2010). Stuff: compulsive Hoarding and the Meaning of Things. New York, NY: Houghton Mifflin Harcourt Publishing.

Fugen, N., Bubrick, J., & Yaryura-Tobias, J.A. (2004). Overcoming Compulsive Hoarding. Oakland, CA: New Harbinger Publications.

Knerr, Phyllis Flood, ed. (2014). The ICD Guide to Collaborating with Professional Organizers. St. Louis, MO, ICD.

Kolberg, Judith, (2013). Getting Organized, in the Era of Endless. Decatur, G. A.: Squall Press.

Mozes, Alan. (2012, August 6). Brain Scans of hoarders Show Unique Abnormalities. Health Day News.

Tolin, D.F., Frost R.O., Steketee G., (2007). Buried in Treasures Help for Compulsive Acquiring, Saving, and Hoarding. New York, NY: Oxford University Press, Inc.

Tompkins, M.A., Hartl, T.L., (2009). Digging Out, Helping your loved one manage clutter, hoarding and compulsive acquiring.Oakland Ca., New Harbinger Publications, Inc.

Journal Articles

Frost, R.O., Patronek, G.,& Rosenfield, W. (2011). A comparison of object and animal hoarding. Depression and Anxiety, 28.

Frost, R.O., Tolin, D.F., Steketee, G., & Oh, M. (2011). Indecisiveness in hoarding. International Journal of Cognitive Therapy, 4, 253-262.

Frost, R.O., Steketee, G., & Tolin, D. F. (2011). Comorbidity in hoarding disorder. Depression and Anxiety, 28, 876-884.

Frost, R.O., Steketee, G., & Tolin, D. F. (2012). Diagnosis and assessment of hoarding disorder. Annual Review of Clinical Psychology, 8, 219-242.

Frost, R.O., & Rasmussen, J. (2011). Phenomenology and characteristics of compulsive hoarding. Chapter 4 in Steketee, G. Oxford Handbook of Obsessive Compulsive and Spectrum Disorders. NY Oxford University Press. Pp. 70-88.

Muroff, J., Steketee, G., Himle, J., Frost, R. (in press) Delivery of internet treatment of compulsive hoarding (D.I.T.C.H.) Behavior Research and Therapy.

Norberg, M.M. Gilliam, C.M., Villavicencio, A., Pearlson, G.D., & Tolin, D.F. (2012). D-cycloserine for treatment nonresponders with obsessive-compulsive disorder A case report. Cognitive and Behavioral Practice. 19, 338-345.

Steketee, G., Gibson, A., Frost, R.O., Alabisco, J., Arluke, A., & Patronek, G. (2011). Characteristics and antecedents of animal hoarding: A comparative interview study. Review of General Psychology, 15, 114-124.

Sorrentino, C., Bratiotis, C., & Muroff, J. (in press). Processes in Group Cognitive & Behavioral Treatment (CBT) for Compulsive Hoarding. Cognitive & Behavioral Practice.

Tolin, D.F., Stevens, M.C., Villavicencio, A.L., Norberg, M.M., Calhoun, V.D., Frost, R.O., et al. (2012). Neural mechanism of decision-making in hoarding disorder. Archives of General Psychiatry, 69, 832-841.

Tolin, D.F., Stevens, M.C., Nave, A.M., Villavicencio, A., & Morrison, S. (2012). Neural mechanisms of cognitive behavioral therapy response in hoarding disorder A pilot study. Journal of Obsessive-Compulsive and Related Disorders, 1, 180-188.

Tolin, D.F., Frost, R.O., & Steketee, G. (2012). Working with hoarding vs. non-hoarding clients a survey of professional's attitudes & experiences. Journal of Obsessive-Compulsive & Related Disorders, 1, 48-53.

Tolin, D.F., Villavicencio, A., Umbach, A. 7 Kurtz, M.M. (2011). Neuropsychological functioning in hoarding disorder. Psychiatry Research, 189, 413-418.

Tolin, D.F., (2011). Understanding & treating hoarding a bio psychosocial perspective. Journal of Clinical Psychology, 67, 517-526.

Web Sites

Anxiety Disorders Association of America: www.adaa.org

Association for Behavioral and Cognitive Therapies: www.abct.org

Heart Centered Hypnotherapy Association: www.wellness-institute.org

EMDR International Association: www.emdria.org

Institute for Challenging Disorganization: www.challenging-disorganization.org

International OCD foundation: www.ocfoundation.org

How to Help a Hoarder: www.howtohelpahoarder.com

National Association of Professional Organizers (NAPO): www.napo.net

International Society for Treatment of Stress Studies www.istss.org

Clutterers Anonymous: www.clutterersanonymous.net

Messies Anonymous: www.messies.com

Listing of Community Hoarding Task forces: www.hoarding-taskforce.com

Children of Hoarders: www.childrenofhoarders.com

Mayo Clinic: www.mayoclinic.org

Dennison & Assoc., Inc.: www.dennisonassociatesinc.com

K2Organizing: www.k2organizing.com

Closing

You now have the tools to help your hoarding and chronically disorganized clients start their new lives. The Fresh Start Group is just that; a START. Your clients will gain the awareness that they are not alone, and they will take the opportunity to learn more about how and why their clutter and hoarding began and continues. Through the Fresh Start Group your clients will create their own mental health and de-cluttering tools and develop a supportive peer community.

End Notes

[1] Kholberg, J. *What Every Professional Organizer Needs to Know About Chronic Disorganization.* Squall Press, DATE

[2] Steketee, G. and Frost, R. O. *Compulsive Hoarding and Acquiring.* Oxford University Press, 2007.

[3] Steketee, G., Frost, R.O., & Kyrios, M. (2003). *Cognitive aspects of compulsive hoarding. Cognitive Therapy and Research,* 27, 463-479.

[4] Tolin, D.F., Frost, R.O., Steketee, G., Gray, K.D., & Firch, K.E. (2008). The economic and social burden of compulsive hoarding. *Psychiatry Research,* 160, 200-211.

[5] Tolin, D.F., Frost, R.O., Steketee, G. (20010). A brief interview for assessing compulsive hoarding: The Hoarding Rating Scale-Interview. *Psychiatry Research,* 178, 147-152.

[6] Hatcher, D. 2010. Retrieved December 2013 from Institute for Challenging Disorganization website, Fact Sheets for the Public page. http://www.challengingdisorganization.org/content/fact-sheets-public-0

[7] Norris, V. 2006. Retrieved December 2013 from Institute for Challenging Disorganization website, Fact Sheets for the Public page. http://www.challengingdisorganization.org/content/fact-sheets-public-0

[8] Institute for Challenging Disorganization Clutter - Hoarding Scale, 2011. Retrieved December 2013 from Institute for Challenging Disorganization website, Resources page. http://www.challengingdisorganization.org/content/clutter-8212-hoarding-scale

[9] Benson, A.L. *Is your client a compulsive buyer? 3 assessment tools for therapists,* 2010.

[10] Neziroglu, Fugen, Bubrick, Jerome, and Yaryura, Jose A. *Overcoming Compulsive Hoarding*. New Harbinger Publications, 2004.

[11] Bourne, Edmund. *The Anxiety and Phobia Workbook*. New Harbinger Publications, 2005.

[12] Tolin, David F., Frost, Randy O., Steketee, Gail. *Buried in Treasures: Help for Compulsive Acquiring, Saving, and Hoarding.* Oxford University Press, 2007.

[13] Tolin, pg. 33. 2007

[14] Tolin, pg. 34. 2007

[15] Tolin, pg. 35. 2007

[16] Tolin, pg. 37. 2007

[17] Retrieved December 2013 from http://en.wikipedia.org/wiki/DISC_assessment

[18] Myers &Briggs Foundation. Retrieved from http://www.myersbriggs.org/my-mbti-personality-type/mbti-basics/ February 28, 2013.

Training and Consultation Opportunities

For up-to-date information on training opportunities, to arrange for a virtual training or a training at your location, and for more information about our training DVD contact us:

Karen Kruzan LISW-S, CPO-CD
161 South Liberty Street
Powell, Ohio 43065, USA
www.k2organizing.com
kkruzan@k2organizing.com
Tel. 614.795.0626

Barbara Jo Dennison PhD, LISW-S
161 South Liberty Street
Powell, Ohio 43065, USA
www.dennisonassociatesinc.com
info@dennisonassociatesinc.com
Tel. 614.888.8440